J
909.1
Medieval world
 Volume 4
 Florence - Hospitals

D1789111

32.50

(1 week che
DATE DU

HESSTON PUBLIC LIBRARY

45560

Medieval World

Volume 4

Florence — Hospitals

GROLIER
EDUCATIONAL

Hesston Public Library
PO Box 640
Hesston, KS 67062

Published by Grolier Educational
Sherman Turnpike
Danbury, Connecticut 06816

© 2001 Brown Partworks Limited

Set ISBN 0-7172-5520-4 (set)
Volume ISBN 0-7172-5524-7

Library of Congress Cataloging-in-Publication Data
Medieval world
    p.cm
  Includes bibliographical references and index.
  Contents: v.1. Abelard–Burgundy—v.2. Byzantine
Empire–Constantinople—v.3. Copts–Feudalism—v.4.
Florence–Hospitals—v.5. House and home–Joan of
Arc—v.6. Justinian–Mediterranean—v.7. Mehmed II–
Painting and sculpture—v.8. Papacy–Roman Empire—
v.9. Rome–Thomas Aquinas—v.10. Tools and
technology–Writing.
  ISBN 0-7172-5520-4 (set)—ISBN 0-7172-5521-2
(v.1)—ISBN 0-7172-5522-0 (v.2)—ISBN 0-7172-
5523-9 (v.3)—ISBN 0-7172-5524-7 (v.4)—ISBN
0-7172-5525-5 (v.5)—ISBN 0-7172-5526-3 (v.6)—
ISBN 0-7172-5527-1 (v.7)—ISBN 0-7172-5528-X
(v.8)—ISBN 0-7172-5529-8 (v.9)—ISBN 0-7172-
5530-1 (v.10)
  1. Middle Ages—Juvenile literature. 2. Civilization,
    Medieval—Juvenile literature. I.
Grolier Educational (Firm)

D117.D37 2001
909'.1—dc21   00-046649

All rights reserved. Except for use in a review, no part of this
book may be reproduced, stored in a retrieval system, or
transmitted in any form, or by any means, electronic, mechanical
photocopying, recording, or otherwise, without prior permission
of Grolier Educational.

For information address the publisher:
Grolier Educational, Sherman Turnpike,
Danbury, Connecticut 06816

FOR BROWN PARTWORKS
Project editor: Sally MacEachern
Designer: Sarah Williams
Picture researcher: Veneta Bullen
Text editor: Chris King
Maps: Mark Walker
Index: Kay Ollerenshaw
Design manager: Lynne Ross
Production manager: Matt Weyland
Managing editor: Tim Cooke
Consultant: Fredric L. Cheyette
                        Amherst College MA

Printed and bound in Singapore

ABOUT THIS BOOK

♦

This set of 10 books tells the stories of the individuals, peoples, battles, treaties, empires, ideas, and religions that shaped the period we call the Middle Ages. When did the Middle Ages begin and end? Historians often suggest that they began in 476, when the last western Roman emperor was deposed by a barbarian chief, and that they ended in 1453, when the Ottoman Turks captured Constantinople, the capital of the eastern Roman empire. These dates, however, are only convenient markers. The Middle Ages were both a continuation of what had gone before, as well as a time of immense social and political change, while advances in architecture, art, literature, and learning paved the way for the period called the Renaissance that began in the 15th century.

The set focuses on Europe, but it also shows how other civilizations such as China, India, and Africa were developing, and the ways in which the Islamic and Christian worlds interacted on many different levels.

The entries in this set are arranged alphabetically and are illustrated with photographs, drawings, and maps. Many of the illustrations come from medieval sources. Each entry ends with a list of cross-references to other entries in the set. They will enable you to find entries on closely related subjects that will help expand and build on your knowledge. At the end of each book there is a timeline to help you relate events to one another in time. There is also a useful "Further Reading" list that includes websites, a glossary of special terms, and an index covering the whole set.

MAPS
The maps in this book show the locations of cities, states and empires in the Middle Ages. However, for the sake of clarity and ease of use, modern place names are often used.

CONTENTS

VOLUME 4

Florence	4
Food and Drink	6
Forests	10
France	12
Francis of Assisi	16
Franks	17
Frederick I	19
Frederick II	20
Friars	21
Gardens	24
Genghis Khan	26
Genoa	27
Germany	29
Glass	33
Government	35
Granada	38
Great Schism	40
Greece	42
Gregory the Great	44
Guilds	45
Hanseatic League	49
Hapsburgs	51
Heaven and Hell	53
Heraldry	55
Heresy	57
Hildegard of Bingen	61
History Writing	62
Holy Roman Empire	63
Horses	65
Hospitals	67
Glossary	*69*
Timeline	*70*
Further Reading	*72*
Set Index	*73*
Picture Credits	*80*

MEDIEVAL WORLD

Florence

The Italian city-state of Florence grew rich and powerful in the Middle Ages through its successful bankers and merchants. A home to many celebrated artists and writers, it later became famous as the birthplace of the Renaissance.

The dome of Florence's cathedral (or Duomo) was designed by the architect Filippo Brunelleschi and built between 1420 and 1436.

Florence was founded as a colony on the Arno River by the Romans in 59 B.C. After the collapse of the Roman Empire in the west Florence was occupied by Ostrogoths, then reconquered by the Byzantines, and finally taken by Lombards. Later the Franks ruled both Florence and Tuscany, the region around it, after they defeated the Lombards in the eighth century. Gradually, local Tuscan chieftains took control. From the 10th century the growing town prospered, and under the rule of Countess Matilda of Tuscany (1046–1115) it gained even more importance. Matilda was a close friend and ally of Pope Gregory VII.

Communal Life

After Matilda's death the city of Florence was run as a commune, which meant that it was governed by elected consuls and made its own regulations. At first only noble families could vote, but later merchants and some craftsmen were also included. During the 13th century the Florentines divided into two parties, Guelfs supporting the authority of the pope, and Ghibellines supporting that of the Holy Roman emperor. The Guelfs eventually triumphed and took control of the city, but they in turn split into feuding factions called Blacks and Whites. The poet Dante was a victim of this bitter feud. He supported the more democratic White Guelfs and had to flee when the Blacks, who were made up of rich merchants, gained control in 1301.

THE MEDICI

The Medici family, who were bankers and merchants, used their great wealth and influence to dominate Florence from the early 15th century. The family's power was first established by Giovanni de' Medici (1360–1429), who made a fortune in banking. His son Cosimo (1389–1464) became chief lender to the city of Florence as well as to the pope. He started the Medici tradition of supporting the arts, asking great artists and sculptors such as Brunelleschi and Donatello to create works especially for him. His grandson Lorenzo (1449–1492), known as "Lorenzo the Magnificent," ruled Florence from 1469. Under him the city achieved its greatest splendor. The pope made Lorenzo's 13-year-old son Giovanni a cardinal. He later became Pope Leo X and a patron of Michelangelo. The Medici continued as grand dukes of Tuscany until the 18th century.

SEE ALSO
♦ Black Death
♦ City-states
♦ Dante
♦ Humanism
♦ Italy
♦ Literature
♦ Painting and Sculpture
♦ Peasant Uprisings
♦ Renaissance

The early decades of the 14th century were a period of exciting growth. The population of the city was approaching 100,000, and the textile industry was thriving. Associations called guilds controlled trade, and the city's chief magistrate could only be selected from among the seven major guilds. Successful banking also brought great wealth.

PLAGUE AND REVOLT

In 1348, however, the Black Death struck and killed at least half of the city's population. Further turmoil came in 1378, when the cloth workers rebelled. The revolt was put down by wealthy merchants and manufacturers. In the late 14th century the Florentines waged wars against rival Italian city-states, such as Pisa and Milan, and built a state that eventually included much of Tuscany.

Florence was home to many great artists and scholars. The poets Boccaccio, Dante, and Petrarch all lived and worked in the city, as did painters and sculptors like Botticelli, Giotto, and Michelangelo. Among the many spectacular pieces of architecture that were built in the medieval period are the Ponte Vecchio bridge and the cathedral, whose dome by Brunelleschi still dominates the city. Some of the great wealth that the city developed was used to support the creative artists who became the driving force behind the cultural explosion of the Renaissance.

Florence is located in northern Italy. In the Middle Ages it was regularly at war with rival Italian cities like Pisa and Milan.

Food and Drink

In medieval Europe the rich ate well, enjoying spectacular feasts consisting of exotic foods. The poor, however, endured a daily diet that was usually dreary and monotonous.

The production, preparation, preservation, and consumption of food were some of the main preoccupations of medieval men and women. While the poor struggled to grow or raise sufficient food for their immediate needs, the rich and the monasteries could produce surplus that could be traded at market.

The most important type of food in medieval Europe was bread. The quality of bread at a meal was an indication of social status. The poorest people ate coarse grains such as oats made into flat pancakes. The next cheapest type of bread, made from ground peas and beans, was called horse bread since it was also fed to horses.

White bread, made from finely ground and sifted wheat flour, was an expensive luxury. The very finest white flour was used to make light pastries, called *simnels*, and the wafers used as the Sacramental Host in the ritual of the Holy Communion.

A baker places a lump of dough into a wood-fueled brick oven. This traditional method of baking bread remained virtually unchanged from the days of the Roman Empire to the 19th century.

Another important staple food for the poor was pottage. It could take the form of a running pottage, which resembled a soup, or a standing pottage, which was more like a thick stew. The main ingredients were vegetables, particularly cabbages, onions, leeks, and garlic. Occasionally meat was also added.

Eating Meat

For most people meat was a luxury. In many countries the rulers passed laws that forbade the poor from hunting wild animals such as deer and boar. Meat from domestic animals, such as beef and pork, was also expensive and was only eaten on special occasions. For the wealthy,

FOOD AND DRINK

however, exotic types of meat provided the basis of extravagant feasts. As well as the beef, pork, and chicken that we eat today, the rich also ate herons, peacocks, venison, wild boar, and even hedgehogs.

However, even the wealthy could not eat meat whenever they wanted. There were religious restrictions as to when people could eat it. Just as Islam and Judaism had strict dietary laws, the Christian church regulated what could be eaten and when. Until the 13th century the church forbade people from eating meat on three days a week. Gradually, the rule was relaxed, and by the 15th century it applied to Fridays only. For these religious purposes meat did not include fish or poultry.

COOKING METHODS

Since animal fats were valuable in the manufacture of candles and soaps, fat rarely made its way into food. Consequently, most medieval food was either boiled or, where possible, baked. Even fruit was cooked—many people believed raw fruit was dangerous. Fish, either fresh or, more often, salted and called *stockfysshe*, was often fried in butter or oil.

THE ENTREMET

One popular feature of the great feasts of the rich was the entremet. It was a visually spectacular display of food like a roasted and decorated boar's head or a peacock that had been removed from its skin with its feathers intact, roasted, and then redressed in its splendid plumage. Another popular entremet was the "four and twenty blackbirds" pie celebrated in the popular nursery rhyme. The live birds would escape and fly around the hall when the pastry crust was broken.

The entremet was heralded into the hall by a fanfare, paraded for the guests to admire, and then received at the head table. Entremets were rarely eaten. Apart from there being very little edible meat, they were considered part of the entertainment rather than the food.

Because food was valuable, very little of it was wasted. Spoiled or rotten food could mean starvation during the winter months, and great time and effort were put into preserving it. The bacteria that make food go bad need moisture to survive, and so most forms of preservation involved ways of removing excess liquid. In warm countries meat and fish could be preserved simply by

Servants prepare a medieval banquet. On the left of the picture a cook carves up pieces of meat. On the right waiters take plates of food to their masters.

ALCOHOLIC DRINKS

Unlike the inhabitants of Islamic states, which had extremely strict rules regarding alcohol, most medieval Europeans drank in great quantities. One of the most popular alcoholic drinks was wine. Because there was a constant need for wine to be used in the communion, the chief winemakers of the Middle Ages were monks. From the 12th century onward French vineyards began to export wine.

Another popular drink was ale, a bitter tasting drink that was made from barley. Ale could be either cloudy or bright depending on its age. The older the ale, the clearer, brighter, and more expensive it was. In Germany herbs were added to ale, while in England it was sweetened with honey.

In England ale was always offered to the lesser guests at feasts, while the expensive, imported wines from France and Germany were reserved for the refined tastes of the wealthy. Middle-ranking guests were served wine mixed with water. Only the guests who sat at the head table were served wine and water separately to mix to their own taste.

This 15th-century illustration shows a woman filling flagons of wine for a wedding celebration.

hanging them out to dry in the sun. Alternatively, meat and fish could be smoked by drying them over a fire. This had the additional benefit of giving the food extra flavor. Another way of preserving food was salting. When it is rubbed into meat, salt removes moisture from it.

Fruits and vegetables could be pickled—stored in jars of salt water or vinegar. However, the lack of fresh fruit available in winter months meant that people did not get the vitamins they needed to protect them from diseases such as scurvy. Generally, the medieval diet lacked many of the vitamins and minerals that are today seen as essential to a healthy lifestyle.

After the Crusaders introduced new foods to Europe, medieval people developed a taste for stronger flavors. Recipes were enhanced by the addition of spices imported from the Middle East. Herbs and spices were sold by apothecaries because they also had medicinal properties. Cooking spices usually came in two varieties: *poudre fort* (strong powder), a mix of black pepper, ginger, cloves, cumin, and other strong spices, and *poudre douce* (soft powder), containing sweeter, milder spices like cinnamon. Other exotic foods that became popular in northern Europe included raisins, dates, and figs from North Africa, Spain, and Portugal.

FOOD COLORINGS

The appearance of food was also important. One of the most widely used colorings was saffron, which turned foods yellow. Rice, the staple diet of India and East Asia, was also grown in Spain and was widely eaten throughout Europe, where it was often served "departed," or divided into two portions of different color.

Wealth did not just determine what people ate: It determined when they ate as well. For ordinary people in the Middle Ages the working day began at dawn. The first and main meal of the day was dinner, which would be eaten around 11:00 A.M. In the summer months, when foods were more plentiful, a light snack finished the day at 4:00 P.M. During winter months, when night set in early, this meal was skipped. The wealthier classes who could afford the luxury of artificial light from candles could extend their day further. Even so, the feasts and banquets of the rich would normally start by noon.

In all households, whether rich or poor, not everyone received the same quantities of food or types of dishes. In poor families the best and largest portions went to the working men. Wives and daughters would often only have what was left over.

In an important and wealthy household the strict hierarchy meant that the lord, his family, and guests at the high table might select from four or five dishes for the first course, while minor guests might have only one or two choices. Except at feasts or banquets, only the head table was served a second course.

> **SEE ALSO**
>
> ♦ Agriculture
> ♦ Daily Life
> ♦ Hunting and Falconry
> ♦ Medicine
> ♦ Trade

A medieval banquet, as shown in an illustration from an 11th-century manuscript. The two men kneeling on either side of the table are servants.

MEDIEVAL WORLD

Forests

The forests that covered much of early medieval Europe were seen as havens of paganism by monks and missionaries, who made great efforts to cleanse them of demons. But they were also filled with natural resources, were easily available to ordinary peasants, and teemed with game.

A painting from the 15th century showing the Italian town of Trento in winter. At the top of the picture workmen are clearing an area of woodland. The timber is then being brought inside the town walls on carts drawn by oxen.

In the early Middle Ages forests re-covered much land that had been cleared in Roman times. Eventually, they covered four-fifths of Europe. In some regions forest and moorland stretched as far as the eye could see. At distant intervals there would be small patches of cleared land on which stood castles, manors, and villages. The forest was both a resource and a limitation. It provided timber, game, and pasture for pigs. However, it was also a seemingly impenetrable barrier to the spread of Christian civilization—especially in central and eastern Europe.

Forest Dangers

While forests were rich in real dangers—ranging from violent outlaws to wild animals—they were also seen as a world of marvelous and frightening legends. Stories of werewolves and other bloodthirsty monsters abounded. People saw forests as places of sorcery and enchantment—pagans believed them to be the home of demons and wood-sprites. As a result, churchmen were suspicious of the forest and sought to control it.

HUNTING IN THE FOREST

The forests were home to a variety of wild animals that could be hunted, such as deer, wild boar, and hare. However, for the poor the business of hunting these animals was extremely risky. In many places the nobility issued laws that gave them an exclusive right to hunt in the forest. In some countries, such as England, these laws were very strictly enforced, and poachers could be executed. Despite these great dangers, illegal hunting continued, with many poor people prepared to risk being caught for the sake of a meal of stewed rabbit.

This illustration from a 14th-century book on hunting shows men armed with spears using a pack of dogs to corner wild boar.

From the 10th century onward the pressures of an increase in population led to a process of deforestation. Villages were founded on newly cleared land. Peasants developed deforestation skills and began to steadily clear away the woods that surrounded their villages.

Reclaiming the Land

The result of the process of deforestation, which was taking place all over Europe, was a huge increase in the amount of land under cultivation. As a result of this revolutionary change the farmers of Europe began to produce a surplus of food. The surplus was available for trade, and this in turn stimulated the growth of towns, markets, and fairs. As more and more buildings were put up, the demand for timber increased, causing people to cut down even greater areas of woodland.

The remaining forests, however, were a rich and much needed resource both for peasants who lived in neighboring villages and for people who made a livelihood from the forest, such as woodcutters and charcoal-burners. In the fall villagers took their pigs into the forests to forage on fallen acorns, fattening them up for the great feasts of the winter. House fires, ovens, and blacksmiths' forges were all hungry for wood or charcoal, which could easily be found in the forest. People used wild berries to supplement their diet, especially in times of hardship. The resin of trees, meanwhile, could be used to make torches and candles.

SEE ALSO

- Agriculture
- Hunting and Falconry
- Magic and Superstition
- Manufacturing

MEDIEVAL WORLD

FRANCE

From 987 to 1589 France was ruled by only two closely related dynasties, the Capetians and the Valois. Under their leadership France eventually became the political and cultural center of western Europe. It was the birthplace of Gothic architecture and the ideals and practices of knighthood. The institutions of government that the Capetians invented were widely imitated, while French became the common language of the nobility from England to the Crusader states of the Holy Land.

In 987, on the death of the Carolingian king Louis V, the great barons of the western Frankish kingdom elected Hugh Capet as their king. Although he and his immediate successors were recognized as king as far away as Catalonia (in modern Spain), their effective area of rule barely extended farther than from Paris to Orléans (on the Loire River), the area known as the Île-de-France. Even at the beginning of the 12th century the king had to use armed force to command the obedience of some of the men who held castles in this area.

Many of the great barons who were the Capetians' neighbors in the

A 15th-century illustration showing the coronation of King Philip II in 1179. Philip greatly expanded the kingdom of France.

later 11th and 12th centuries had greater wealth and could command larger armies than the king. Among the most important of them were the counts of Anjou, Champagne, and Flanders. Another was the duke of Normandy, who became king of England in 1066.

THE ANGEVIN EMPIRE

Between 1153 and 1169 the count of Anjou greatly increased the territory under his control. By a combination of marriage and armed conquest, he acquired Normandy, Brittany, Aquitaine, and England, becoming King Henry II (ruled 1154–1189). He also married his son John to the heiress of an Alpine county, giving him control of a major pass into Italy. This collection of lands is sometimes called the Angevin Empire. Although Henry II and his sons recognized the Capetians as their overlords, they were constantly at war with Louis VII (ruled 1137–1180) and Philip II (ruled 1179–1223).

Though weaker by far than the Angevins who controlled the entire western half of what is now France, the Capetians had the title of king and used it astutely to increase their territories. Louis VI (ruled 1108–1137) and Louis VII asserted their rights as protectors of bishops and monasteries within the lands of their great barons. Churchmen who lived beyond the borders of the king's own lands could appeal to the king's court if they believed that they had been wronged.

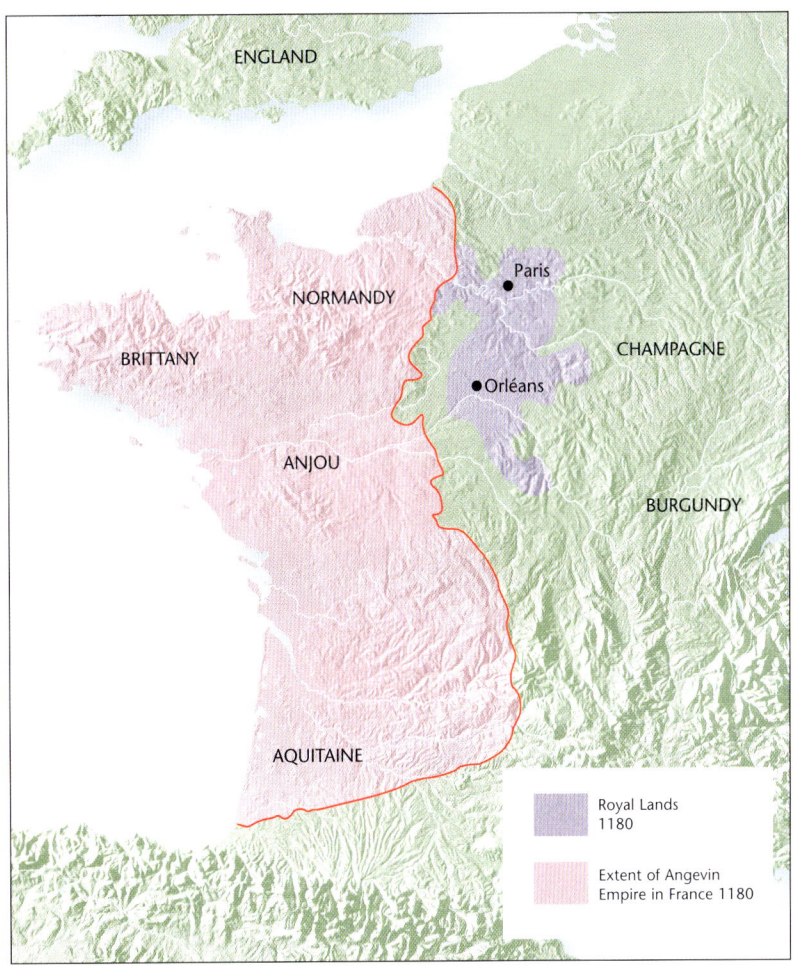

In the 12th century the kingdom of France was dwarfed by the neighboring Angevin Empire.

THE SALIC LAW

When Charles IV died in 1328, he had no son to succeed him. His only living sibling was Isabella, wife of Edward II of England. Rather than risk having Edward become their king, the French barons elected Philip of Valois, the nephew of Philip IV. When the English kings claimed to be legitimate kings of France by descent from Isabella, French lawyers invented the Salic Law, so named because they claimed it was a law of the Salian Franks. It ruled that no woman could take the crown of France, nor anyone whose descent from a legitimate king was only through a woman. This rule remained a fundamental law of the French monarchy until the 18th century.

Philip II (ruled 1179–1223) used an appeal to his court to eliminate the Angevin threat in the north. In 1202, when King John refused to stand trial in Philip's court on charges brought by one of his subjects, Philip confiscated all the Angevin lands and with swift military action conquered all their lands north of the Loire River. Aquitaine, however, remained in English hands. Disputes over the powers of the French kings to hear appeals from people from Aquitaine eventually became one of the major causes of the Hundred Years' War.

Philip later allowed his son to take over the leadership of the Albigensian Crusade. The crusade brought all of southern France between the Rhone and Aquitaine under royal rule. Most of the easternmost territories of modern France, however, were only acquired much later, some as late as the 19th century.

This bronze statue of King Louis IX stands in the U.S. city that bears his name, St. Louis. Louis helped establish a centralized system of government.

GOVERNMENT

To administer their newly acquired lands, Philip II and his successors appointed professional officials, called bailiffs in the north and seneschals in the south. They were assisted by judges and had a small police force. Louis IX (ruled 1226–1270) created a central royal judicial court, called the Parlement, staffed by university-trained lawyers. A central financial administration began with the creation of the Chamber of Accounts in 1320. These institutions were staffed partly by clergy and partly by laymen. Through loyal work for the king these officials sometimes earned noble status.

Before the late 15th century there was no permanent army or navy. When war threatened, the king summoned his nobility to fight, but the major block of fighting men were mercenaries. To pay for these fighting men, the king needed to collect taxes. Philip IV (ruled 1285–1314) and his successors began to summon local and regional assemblies of townsmen and nobles, called "Estates," to explain their needs and get consent to collect these taxes. On rare occasions a single assembly, known as the "Estates General," was called for the entire kingdom.

FRANCE

A 14th-century illustration showing a fair held at St. Denis, Paris. Trading fairs were held regularly throughout the year.

Eventually, some of the regional Estates also developed small administrative staffs.

KING AND CHURCH

Churchmen always played important roles in medieval royal courts. Before the late 13th century laymen were rarely literate, so clergy were required to perform tasks involving reading and writing or the use of Latin. Unlike the English kings, those of France could not appoint people directly to church offices, but they could recommend those they favored to the church bodies that had the right of election or appointment. They could also make their recommendations to the pope, who from the late 13th century onward claimed the right to appoint many church offices. Many men made their career in royal service before becoming bishops or cardinals.

When Philip IV attempted to tax churchmen and church property to support his wars, he came into conflict with Pope Boniface VIII (pope 1294–1303). The pope threatened to excommunicate Philip, denying him the right to take part in church rituals. In retaliation Philip accused Boniface of heresy and witchcraft, and sent an armed band to arrest him and bring him to trial. He also launched a propaganda campaign against the pope. Boniface died soon after the attack. The popes who followed were more flexible with royal demands and regularly granted the king the right to tax the clergy. In 1309 Pope Clement V even moved the papal residence to Avignon, just across the Rhone River from France.

TRADE

One of the most important trade routes in Europe passed through eastern France, along the Rhone and Saône Rivers to Champagne and Flanders. This route connected the thriving commercial cities of Italy, such as Genoa, Pisa, and Florence, to the industrial cities of the Low Countries.

The ordinary rural market, usually held once a week for trading of local products, was not big or important enough for foreign merchants. In the 12th century a new feature of commerce led to a dramatic increase in trade. It was the regional fair. Most often it took the endorsement of a local duke to set up one of these fairs, since he could protect the traders from the threat of robbers. Each fair lasted from a few days up to six weeks, and merchants could move from one to another throughout the year.

The largest and most popular fairs were in the county of Champagne, strategically located for travel in all directions. Six fairs were held a year in Champagne, the largest two at Troyes and Provins.

SEE ALSO

- Angevins
- Burgundy
- Capetians
- Cathedrals
- Eleanor of Aquitaine
- Fairs and Markets
- Franks
- Great Schism
- Hundred Years' War
- Papacy
- Paris
- Parliaments
- Phlip IV

Francis of Assisi

Francis of Assisi (1182–1226) was the founder of the Franciscan order of friars in the Roman Catholic church. He lived a life of Christlike poverty and is popularly known for his love of nature.

Born in 1182 in the Italian town of Assisi, Francis was christened Giovanni Bernardone, but was known by the nickname his father gave him, Francesco. Francesco's father was a wealthy textile merchant, and he saw to it that his son received a good education.

Francis had a colorful early life. He joined the army to fight for Assisi against the neighboring city of Perugia, but was captured and held prisoner for a year. After a pilgrimage to Rome he had a vision telling him to rebuild a ruined church near Assisi. He then sold all his worldly goods plus a large amount of his father's belongings to fund the building project. Francis's actions greatly angered his father, who publicly disowned him.

Francis began to live by begging. He preached poverty and brotherly love, cared for the sick, and soon had a group of followers. He also wrote a book of guidance for his disciples to follow known as the *Regula Primitiva* (Primitive Rule). In 1209 Pope Innocent III approved the group as the Friars Minor.

The Little Brothers

Francis intended that his "little brothers" work to support themselves; but since they spent more time with the poor and sick, they were increasingly supported by charitable donations. They undertook extensive preaching missions trying to convert people to the Roman Catholic church.

By 1223 the group had grown considerably, and Francis no longer felt capable of administrating it. He gradually withdrew from leadership. Living in solitude, he spent much time in prayer. During this time Francis wrote the poem "Canticle to the Sun," urging people to live in harmony with nature. He saw all living creatures as his "brothers" and was famous for his love of animals.

Francis died in Assisi in 1226. He was made a saint by Pope Gregory IX two years later.

This 14th-century portrait of Saint Francis is in the Church of San Francesco in Assisi. Work on the church began in 1228, the year that Francis was made a saint.

SEE ALSO
- Charity
- Church
- Friars

Franks

The Franks were a Germanic tribe that invaded western Europe in the fifth century A.D. Their history can be divided into two almost equal segments: the Merovingian era from 481 to 751 and the Carolingian age from 751 to 987.

A 16th-century book illustration showing Pippin III being crowned king of the Franks by Archbishop Boniface at Soissons in 751. Three years later he was officially crowned by Pope Stephen II.

During the declining years of the western Roman Empire two groups of Franks, the Ripuarians and the Salians, migrated west into the areas that the Romans called Belgica and Gallia. In 481, 15-year-old Clovis (466–511) became king of the Salians. By 486 he had completely routed all opposition.

Claiming to be the rightful heir of a previous king, Merovech, Clovis executed rival claimants to the throne, made a peace treaty with the neighboring Burgundians, and crushed all enemy tribes. By 510 he had succeeded in forging a huge empire—known as Francia.

FIGHTING TACTICS

The military success of the Franks in Clovis's time was due partially to the ferocity of their warriors and partially to their unique tactics. The Franks ran into battle in a seemingly disorganized mass, throwing heavy battleaxes into the enemy ranks. In the confusion the Franks then rushed in and finished off their opponents with swords.

Under Charlemagne Frankish fighting methods changed considerably, increasingly revolving around the use of heavy cavalry. A typical Frankish knight wore heavy chain mail and was armed with both a lance and a sword. In battle the knights charged at the enemy in close formation, usually scattering their more lightly armed opponents.

This highly romanticized 19th-century painting by Charles Steuben shows Charles Martel leading his army to victory against Muslim forces at the Battle of Tours in 732. Martel is mounted on the white horse.

When Clovis made his treaty with the king of the Burgundians, part of the agreement was that he would marry the king's daughter, Clotilda (about 470–545). Their marriage in about 492 proved to be the most significant event of Clovis's reign. Clotilda persuaded her husband to adopt Roman Christianity, not the Arian form practiced by the Visigoths. Clovis's conversion created an important alliance of the Franks with the pope.

On Clovis's death in 511 the kingdom was divided. The subsequent history of the Merovingians is one of civil war and constant conflict. Government was conducted by provincial administrators and royal officials. The most important of them was the mayor of the palace.

After the death of Dagobert I in 639 a series of weak kings opened the way for powerful mayors to rise in importance. The strongest was Charles Martel (about 688–741), who became mayor in 716. He subdued all rivals, conquered the Frisians, Saxons, and all Germanic tribes eastward to the Slavic borders, then turned westward to face the invasions of the North African Muslims who had conquered Spain and advanced as far north as the Loire River in France. There, at the Battle of Tours in 732, Charles halted a Muslim raiding force.

Charles Martel's son, Pippin III (about 714–768), was determined to replace the title of mayor with that of king. To do so, he sought the blessing of the pope, who in turn was looking for allies in his struggle against the Lombards in Italy. In 754 the Pope crowned Pippin king. In 756 Pippin defeated the Lombards and presented the conquered territory to the pope as "the Donation of Pippin." These lands eventually formed the basis of the Papal States, over which the pope had power.

CHARLEMAGNE

The Carolingian era in Frankish history began with Pippin's successor Charlemagne (742–814). This period was the pinnacle of Frankish power and achievement. Charlemagne defeated the Lombards, Bavarians, and Saxons, creating a huge empire that reached from the Atlantic Ocean to the Saale River in Germany. On Christmas Day 800 Pope Leo III crowned Charlemagne emperor, the effect of which was to solidify the alliance of the Franks with the Roman Catholic church.

Charlemagne's empire did not remain intact for long after his death. By the Treaty of Verdun in 843 his grandsons divided the territory into three separate areas. This division of the empire opened the way for attacks by bands of marauding Vikings. By the end of the 10th century the days of the great Carolingian empire had come to an end.

SEE ALSO

♦ Barbarian Invasions
♦ Burgundy
♦ Charlemagne
♦ Feudalism
♦ France

FREDERICK I

Frederick I (about 1122–1190), known as Barbarossa or "Red Beard," was king of Germany and Holy Roman emperor. During his reign he had a long struggle for power with the pope and was successful in unifying the German principalities.

Frederick was the son of the Duke of Swabia and the Duke of Bavaria's daughter, which made him a descendant of two powerful rival families—the Welfs and the Hohenstaufens. People of both duchies and other German regions thought that Frederick could unite the regions of Germany, and he was elected king in 1152. He promised Pope Adrian IV that his army would protect the pope from potential enemies such as the Normans of southern Italy. In return Adrian crowned him emperor in 1155.

BATTLES WITH THE POPE

In the disputed papal elections of 1159 Frederick supported Victor IV. Victor's rival, Alexander III, was finally recognized by most of Europe. He excommunicated Frederick, denying him the right to take part in church rituals. Over the next 16 years Frederick launched a series of attacks on Italy, but in 1176 he lost the decisive Battle of Legnano to the Lombard League of northern Italian cities. After this setback he reconciled himself with Alexander.

Frederick recognized the power and independence of the nobles who ruled the German principalities. He also issued legislation in imitation of the ancient Roman emperors. In 1189 Frederick organized the Third Crusade to free Jerusalem from the Muslims. He rode with his knights on the Crusade, but drowned while crossing a river on his way to the Holy Land.

The German people greatly admired Frederick. According to a famous legend, he is still alive and sleeps beside a huge table in a cave in the Kyffhäuser Mountains in Germany. When his red beard has grown three times around the table, the legend says, Frederick will wake up and rule over his empire again.

This bronze head of Frederick I was originally made to hold a relic of Saint John the Evangelist. It was made during the 12th century and is now in the German town of Cappenberg.

SEE ALSO

♦ Crusades
♦ Germany
♦ Holy Roman Empire

FREDERICK II

Frederick II (1194–1250) was Holy Roman emperor and king of Germany and Sicily. He was a highly capable politician and soldier who also took a great interest in science, languages, and the arts.

Frederick was the son of Henry VI of Germany and Constance of Sicily. He was the grandson of Frederick I. At the age of two Frederick was elected king by the German princes; he became king of Sicily when he was three. When the young Frederick's parents died, Pope Innocent III became his guardian.

In Germany two rival kings, Philip of Swabia and Otto IV, were soon elected in Frederick's place. The young king's grip on Sicily was equally precarious, and for years rival forces fought for power. However, in 1209 Frederick married Constance of Aragon. Her knights helped him gain control of Sicily. In 1212 he reconquered southern Germany, finally defeating Otto in 1214.

Frederick had many difficulties and arguments with the pope. But in 1220 he promised to support Pope Honorius III, and the pope crowned him Holy Roman emperor in Rome. The pope expected Frederick to organize a crusade to free the Holy Land from Muslims. He eventually set out in 1228. However, rather than trying to conquer them, Frederick made treaties with the Arabs. These treaties brought Jerusalem and Bethlehem under Christian control.

This illustration of Frederick II comes from his own work *The Art of Falconry*. The book took him 30 years to write and is still used by falconers today.

Under Frederick's rule Sicily blossomed. The region became an important center of trade. Artists and scholars came from all over Europe and the Arab world. Thanks to Frederick's respect for Islamic culture, Sicily became a place where ideas could be exchanged between the Arab and Christian worlds.

When Frederick died in 1250, many assumed that his empire would live on through his heirs. But 22 years later Frederick's line died out.

SEE ALSO

- Crusades
- Germany
- Holy Roman Empire
- Islamic Scholarship
- Italy

Friars

The word "friar" comes from the French word *frére*, which means "brother." A friar was a member of one of the so-called mendicant, or begging, orders established by the Roman Catholic church.

In the 13th century the church was a great landowner. It possessed enormous monasteries and cathedrals, collected large amounts of money in tithes and taxes, and was heavily involved in political and military affairs throughout Europe. A common feature of the medieval church was that whenever it became too involved with the affairs of the world, new groups would emerge who would look back to the original teachings of Christ. Such was the case with the friars.

Mendicant Orders

The friars, or "mendicants" (from the Latin word *mendicare*, meaning "to beg"), were men who refused to accept a regular income and instead took a vow of poverty. They were distinguished from monks in that monks withdrew from the world, living inside a monastery, while friars traveled out from their friary and worked actively among the people.

Supported by alms (charitable donations), friars ministered as needed in towns and villages. When not preaching the Bible, they spent much of their time tending to the sick and the poor. The work of the friars injected new life into the Christian faith at a time when the church was becoming increasingly out of touch with the concerns and lives of ordinary people.

The five best-known orders of friars were the Franciscans, Dominicans, Carmelites, Augustinians, and Servites. The Franciscans were the first mendicant order to be established. The order was led by Francis of Assisi (1182–1226), who wrote a book of rules for his disciples to follow. It advocated a life of Christlike simplicity and absolute poverty. He appealed to Pope Innocent III for support, which was granted in 1209. So was born the "Order of Friars Minor." The friars focused mainly on preaching the gospel and acts of charity.

A panel from a 13th-century fresco showing Pope Innocent III giving his approval to Saint Francis, so authorizing the formation of the Order of Friars Minor.

SAINT DOMINIC

Dominic was born in about 1170 in a village in Castile in Spain. At age seven he went to live with his uncle, who was a priest. As a teenager Dominic began to study theology. He became a distinguished scholar and was also known for his acts of charity toward the poor.

In 1203 Dominic accompanied the Bishop of Osma to southern France, where he came into contact with the Albigensians. The Albigensians were a heretical group who believed the Roman church to be corrupt and overly wealthy. Dominic realized that it would be easier to win people back to the official Christian faith by preaching from a position of poverty. With this object in mind he founded the Dominican order in 1216. Dominic traveled widely across Europe preaching the gospel, and on a missionary trip to Hungary in 1221 he fell sick and died. He was made a saint in 1234 by Pope Gregory IX.

As the order grew in size, Francis's original rule proved too strict. Its insistence on absolute poverty was impractical since the order needed monastic houses as bases for its friars. A new, more relaxed rule was introduced in 1223, but it was not enough to stop an eventual split in the ranks of the order. One group, known as the Spirituals, tried to go back to the spirit of Francis's original intentions. Another, called the Conventuals, took a more moderate approach.

THE DOMINICANS

Officially known as the Order of Friars Preachers, the Dominicans took their name from their founder Saint Dominic (about 1170–1221). The Dominicans were famous for providing education for common people. They settled in Europe's intellectual centers and soon dominated the departments of theology in major universities such as Oxford and Paris. Their scholars produced many impressive philosophical works.

Because of their great knowledge Dominicans were often chosen by the popes to serve as inquisitors to search out and suppress heresy. They extended their missionary work to the farthest corners of the earth: In 1272 a delegation preached to the court of Kublai Khan in northern China, and in the early 1500s their most famous missionary, Bartolemé de las Casas (1474–1566), preached to the native inhabitants of Central America.

THE CARMELITES

The Carmelites were founded in 1155 by a monk who organized a group of hermits living on Mount Carmel in Palestine. They were supported by Pilgrims coming to the Holy Land. When the tide of the Crusades turned against the Europeans, the Carmelites moved to Europe.

In 1245 the Carmelites held a meeting in England, where they chose as their "general" the 80-year-old Simon Stock. Despite his age, Simon led them for the next 20 years. During that time, at his urging, the Carmelites became a mendicant order and were authorized by Pope Innocent IV in 1247.

The Carmelites now adopted a new habit: a white robe and a gray scapula. A scapula is a small garment worn over the robe and made of two horizontal strips of cloth joined by cords over the shoulders. According to Carmelite tradition, this emblem was given to Simon Stock by the Virgin Mary, who promised to rescue from purgatory all who were wearing it at the time of their death. The Carmelites reached the highpoint of their influence in the mid-1600s.

The fourth major order of mendicants were the Augustinians, or Austin Friars, who wore black robes and hoods. They were founded in 1244, when Pope Innocent IV brought together a number of scattered groups of monks known as Austin Hermits. These monks followed the teachings of Saint Augustine of Hippo (354–430). The Augustinian order grew rapidly and before the end of the 15th century numbered about 30,000 members. Much of the work of the Augustinians was educational.

THE SERVITES

The Servites originated as a group of seven men from Florence who withdrew to an area outside the city to live a life of poverty. In 1233 they took up a uniform of hairshirt and gray robe, changed in 1256 at the time of their authorization by Pope Alexander IV to a white robe, black hood and scapular, and a leather girdle. They were also known as the Brothers of the Passion of Jesus.

In 1304 a parallel group for women, the "Black Sisters," was organized, devoted to the care of the poor and sick and to the education of young children. The Servites spread quickly throughout Italy, France, Germany, Holland, Poland, and Hungary, and shortly after 1350 they were engaged in mission work as far away as India. By that time they were recognized as the fifth most important order of mendicants.

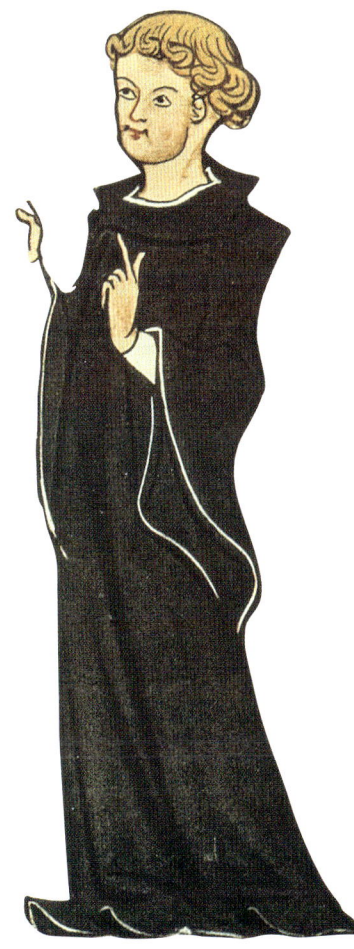

A Dominican novice friar with his abbot. The Dominicans were founded in 1216. They soon grew to dominate the universities of medieval Europe.

SEE ALSO

- Charity
- Francis of Assisi
- Heresy
- Inquisition
- Missionaries
- Religious Thought and Philosophy
- Thomas Aquinas

MEDIEVAL WORLD

Gardens

In the Middle Ages gardens were important sources of food and medicine, as well as places of quiet contemplation and religious meditation. While the poor had small plots of land on which they grew vegetables, enclosed gardens were found exclusively on the grounds of the monasteries and near the large houses of the nobility.

A 14th-century book illustration showing people picking medicinal flowers in an herb garden.

While formal enclosed gardens were common in ancient Rome, they largely disappeared from western Europe after Germanic tribes overran the empire in the fifth century. In the early medieval period such formal gardens were found on the grounds of monasteries. Since monasteries were often left undisturbed during wars and periods of civil strife, many of their account books containing lists of plants, their uses, and the methods of gardening have survived.

European monasteries favored the courtyard garden, which was enclosed by a wall. This rectangular piece of land was often divided into four beds by pathways. These paths formed the shape of a cross, at the center of which was a fountain or water-tank. By the walls of the monastery chapel was a circular bed called the paradise. That is where the monks would go to pray quietly, and where flowers were grown for the garlands used to decorate saints' shrines and statues on feast days.

Herbal Remedies

Since it usually fell to the monks to treat the sick, there was also a garden where medicinal herbs were grown. The monks used the herb feverfew to treat headaches. They also believed that rosemary warded off disease and used this herb to purify the air in their hospitals.

The larger monasteries also had a cellarer's garden where the *gruit* (bitter) herbs used to flavor ales were grown. The monks of some orders became famous for their herb-based liqueurs, such as the yellow or green-colored Chartreuse made by the Carthusian monks near Grenoble, France.

DRY GARDENS

In 15th-century Japan a style of garden grew up that was completely different from anything that appeared in the West: the dry garden. These enclosures usually featured no plants or water: Instead, they were made up of rocks and gravel. The rocks were arranged so that they resembled mountains and waterfalls, while the gravel was raked into designs that represented flowing water.

Such gardens were found mainly in Buddhist monasteries. They were designed for silent contemplation by monks, and raking the patterns formed part of their rituals. One of the most famous examples is the Ryoan-ji garden in the Daisen-in Monastery in Kyoto.

The garden of the Zuiho-in Monastery in Kyoto, Japan, is an example of a dry garden. The gravel is raked neatly into lines.

In the 13th century similar gardens began to appear on the grounds of the large houses of the nobility. The communal nature of medieval life encouraged the development of private, ornamental gardens for the exclusive use of the rich. These gardens were designed to provide as relaxing an environment as possible. They often featured benches set into their walls and shaded pathways. During the summer flowers grew.

In Christian doctrine the enclosed garden grew to be associated with the Virgin Mary. The garden represented her virginity, while the flowers and fruits symbolized her "flowering" as the mother of Christ. Nonreligious manuscripts and paintings celebrated the enclosed garden as the home of the troubadour, the noble poet who devoted himself to his virtuous lady with a pure and selfless love.

Gardens were even more highly valued in the hot countries of the Islamic world. Traditionally, Islamic gardens were calm and cool sanctuaries away from the searing heat and dust of the towns and countryside. Water, a scarce and precious commodity in daily life, was an important feature. It demonstrated that the owner of the garden had access to his own private water supply and was thus extremely wealthy. The word "paradise" is derived from the Persian word *pairidaeza*, meaning "enclosure."

SEE ALSO

♦ Courtly Love
♦ Hospitals
♦ House and Home
♦ Islam
♦ Japan
♦ Medicine
♦ Monasteries

Medieval World

Genghis Khan

Genghis Khan rose to lead the nomadic Mongol tribes of western Central Asia in the early 13th century and waged many wars to create a vast empire that stretched from the Pacific to eastern Europe.

Genghis Khan (about 1162–1227) succeeded his father, the chief of a local Mongol tribe, at the age of 13 and successfully defended his people from attack by neighboring tribes. He next began to unite the various warring Mongol tribes under his leadership. In 1206 he abandoned his given name, Temujin, and took the title Genghis Khan, meaning "Universal Ruler," reflecting the new unity of the Mongol people.

Over the following years Genghis greatly expanded his kingdom. In 1211 he overran much of northern China and five years later took control of the area lying around Lake Balkhask and Tibet. Pushing further westward, the khan's forces took over the empire of Khwarezm, which stretched from the Caspian Sea to the Persian Gulf, in 1220 and 1221. Genghis returned to his capital, Karakorum, in 1225, but his generals continued his conquests, advancing into southern Russia and the Crimean Peninsula, and completing the occupation of northern China by 1223. Genghis died in 1227 after a further attack on China.

Genghis Khan was known throughout the medieval world for his ruthlessness and cruelty—he once had 70 enemy chieftains boiled alive. However, he was also an excellent administrator and skilled negotiator, and was willing to adopt aspects of other cultures. His deeds laid the foundation for the largest empire the world has ever seen.

Genghis Khan leads his army in an attack on an enemy fortress.

SEE ALSO

- China
- Marco Polo
- Mongols
- Tamerlane
- Warfare

Genoa

Genoa, on the northwest coast of Italy, was an important port during the Middle Ages. At the height of its influence in the 13th century it was the center of a huge trading network that stretched throughout the Mediterranean and into Asia as far as China.

This painting of the harbor of Genoa dates from the late 15th century. By that time Genoa's power and influence were in decline.

The port of Genoa was founded in ancient times as a small fishing village. Eventually, the Romans began using it for their fleet. After the fall of the western Roman Empire in the fifth century, however, Genoa suffered a number of attacks from Germanic tribes. The town was sacked in 642, and the Genoese set about improving their defenses by building walls and becoming a strong naval power.

In the 10th century Genoa faced a new problem: attack by Muslims based on the islands of Corsica and Sardinia and in northern Africa. This time the Genoese counterattacked and made an alliance with the port of Pisa to help against further Muslim raids. Before long, Genoese merchant ships were trading with other Mediterranean ports, and the city was growing in wealth. Until around 1100 Genoa was ruled by its bishop. On the eve of the First Crusade the most influential citizens formed an association called a *compagna*, whose officials were called consuls. Eventually, these elected consuls became the government of the city.

During the 12th and 13th centuries the Crusades helped Genoa grow. The city supplied many of the ships and equipment needed to take Christian knights to the Holy Land. As a result of the First Crusade

THE FIESCHI

Among the most important noble Genoese families were the Fieschi. Their period of greatest influence began when Sinibaldo Fieschi became pope in 1243, taking the name Innocent IV. This meant that in the great political battle of the 13th century the family supported the Guelf faction on the side of the pope against the Ghibelline faction, which supported the Holy Roman emperor.

At this time Genoa was governed by "captains of the people" with the support of the guilds. The Fieschi plotted against these rulers and were exiled. They were soon back, however, and allied themselves with the French prince Charles of Anjou. Over the next few centuries the Fieschi served as ambassadors and soldiers, playing an active role in the politics of both Genoa and other Italian cities.

(1095–1099) the Genoese obtained special trading privileges with the port of Acre (in modern Israel). They also began to establish trading colonies all around the Mediterranean. Some were set up by peaceful bargaining, while others were the result of more aggressive campaigning. At the same time, Genoa took control of the surrounding countryside in the region of Liguria, as well as parts of Corsica and Sardinia.

AN EXPANDING CITY

As trade increased and the port became busier, Genoa's population grew to about 100,000. In the 13th century Genoa competed with Venice for trade in the Byzantine Empire, and the Genoese set up trading settlements on the coast of the Black Sea. They even had their own independent quarter in the Byzantine capital of Constantinople. As sea trade reached its peak, Genoa's rivalry with Pisa over Sardinia led to a naval battle in 1284, which Genoa won.

In the 14th century Genoa's importance declined. At home there were political struggles within the city as ruling families competed with each other for power. In 1339 Genoa tried to stop disagreements within the city by appointing a doge (or chief magistrate) in the style of the Venetians, but this was not successful. Matters were made worse by a series of disasters. In the middle of the 14th century the Black Death claimed tens of thousands of lives in Genoa. Then wars with Venice for control of trade in the eastern Mediterranean resulted in defeat in 1381. Thirteen years later France took over the city, and then Milan gained control for some years. Genoa was no longer a great power, and its glorious medieval period was over.

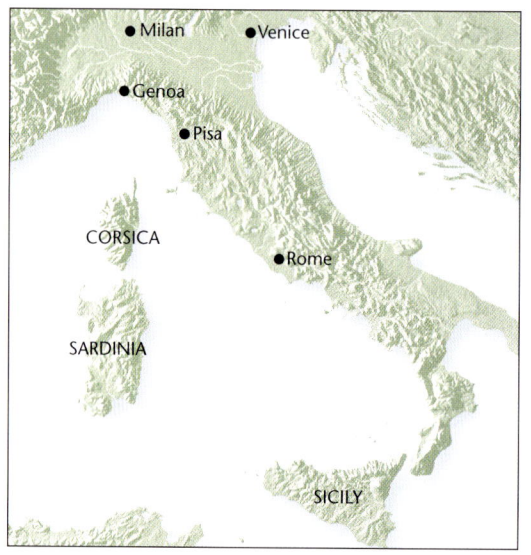

Genoa is located on the northwest coast of Italy. During the Middle Ages it became the center of a vast trading empire that stretched all across the Mediterranean.

SEE ALSO

♦ Black Death
♦ Crusades
♦ Holy Roman Empire
♦ Italy
♦ Ships and Seafaring
♦ Trade
♦ Venice

GERMANY

At the beginning of the Middle Ages Germany as we know it did not exist. The land the Romans knew as Germania, a vast region east of the Rhine and north of the Danube Rivers, was vaguely defined. As the Middle Ages went on, however, it gradually began to assume a distinct identity of its own.

The people who lived in Germania spoke a common language. Around 500 A.D Germanic-speakers were divided into a number of tribes. Among the most important were the Goths, Alemans, Franks, Saxons, and Lombards. The Franks moved westward and formed a kingdom in what had been Roman Gaul; it later became modern France. Although the Franks were heavily outnumbered in Gaul, they conquered all local rivals and soon gave their name to the region—Francia.

CHARLEMAGNE

Early Frankish kings intervened occasionally in Germania, but they did not make it a part of their kingdom. A decisive turning point came in the eighth century, when the Frankish ruler Charlemagne (742–814) conquered a northern region of Germania called Saxony and made it Christian. In the ninth and 10th centuries Saxony played a leading role in the emerging German realm. Equally importantly, Charlemagne's armies defeated the Turkic-speaking Avars who lived in the Carpathian Basin, in modern Hungary, a region that had been occupied by fierce nomads for centuries.

Following this conquest Charlemagne went to Rome, where he was crowned emperor by the pope on Christmas Day, 800. In this way he revived the idea of a western Roman Empire. Charlemagne's kingdom included much of modern Germany, as well as France, Italy, and the Low Countries. However, the great empire created by Charlemagne

This 15th-century painting by the German artist Albrecht Dürer shows the Frankish king Charlemagne. His empire covered much of modern-day Germany and France. The black eagle of Germany can be seen in the top left of the picture.

lasted only until the death of his son Louis the Pious in 840. It was then divided into three regions. The area that lay to the east of the Rhine River became the East Frankish kingdom, the forerunner of modern Germany.

At the end of the ninth century Magyars, mounted archers from the Eurasian steppes, occupied the former territory of the Avars in the Carpathian Basin, from where they launched raids into western Europe. Finally, in 955 the German king Otto I (912–973) destroyed a large Magyar army in battle at Lechfeld. Otto gained much prestige as a result of this victory. It freed western Europe from the menace of steppe warriors for several centuries and paved the way for the economic development of Germany and central Europe. Otto also acquired the title of king of Italy, and in 962 he was crowned Roman emperor.

HOLY ROMAN EMPIRE

Subsequently, rulers of the region were crowned as kings of Germany and then crossed the Alps for another coronation in Rome, where they claimed the title emperor. Despite their imperial Roman title, these rulers, with a few notable exceptions, lived in northern Europe. For this reason the vast territory that they governed is sometimes known as the German empire. The official term Holy Roman Empire dates from the mid-12th century. In the 14th century this realm became known as the Holy Roman Empire of the German Nation, which reflected a developing sense of German identity.

However, the German kings of the 11th and 12th centuries were often not as powerful as they seemed. No dynasty ever succeeded in gaining undisputed possession of the crown for long. Germany was governed mostly on a local level by princes, dukes, and bishops. These local rulers elected the king and were sometimes more powerful than him. Also, no capital city emerged in medieval Germany, partially because the various ruling dynasties had differing centers of power. In contrast with the rulers of France, who were firmly anchored in Paris, German kings continually moved from city to city. Historians call this method of ruling itinerant kingship.

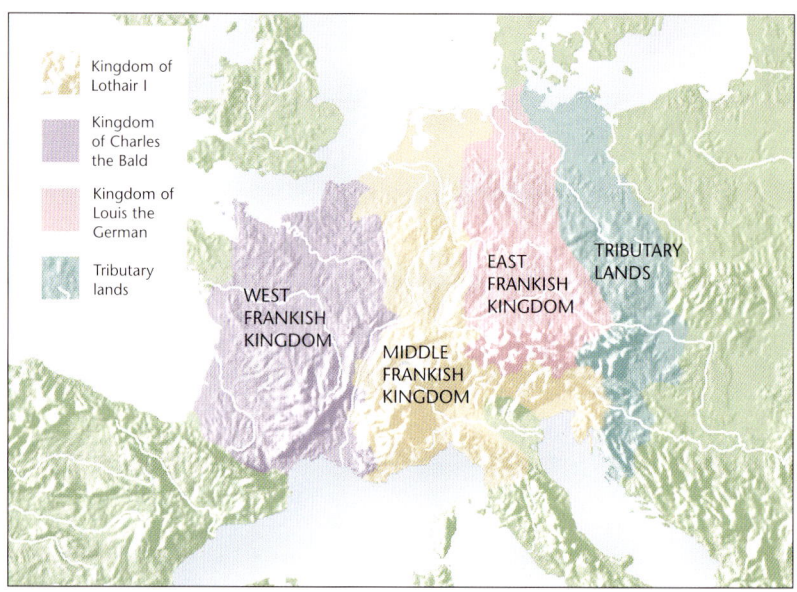

In many respects medieval Germany emerged because of the interactions between Latin Christianity in the west and the pagan or newly converted populations of east-central Europe. Often these interactions came in the form of military conquests that were followed by forced political, economic, and religious integration. On the other hand, the use of military power frequently failed, but the populations of east-central Europe eventually accepted Christianity from their western neighbors anyway and even invited Germanic-speakers into their territories.

After the death of Louis the Pious in 840 the Frankish nation divided into three separate regions, each ruled by one of his sons. The East Frankish kingdom, together with the lands that paid tribute to it, formed the basis of modern Germany.

THE RISE OF THE MINISTERIALS

Germany was dominated politically and socially by imperial aristocrats who traced their ancestries back to Charlemagne. They competed fiercely with one another for official positions and even for the kingship, but they needed help in governing. In the 11th century a social class of servants called ministerials became increasingly important in government and war. These men, who were legally serfs, served their masters as soldiers and administrators, and some became rich and powerful. Many were extremely well-educated, yet they were never really accepted as equals by those of illustrious ancestry. The ministerials Wolfram von Eschenbach, Walter von der Vogelweide, Hartmann von Aue, and Ulrich von Lichtenstein became major poets. Their works offer a running commentary on German society and culture.

This 14th-century book illustration shows the poet Walter von der Vogelweide meditating. Walter specialized in love poetry, but his work also touched on religious and political themes.

For example, Charlemagne conquered and converted large portions of the Carpathian Basin. However, East Frankish rulers lost control over this region as Hungarians settled there in the 10th century; and despite Otto I's decisive victory at Lechfeld, German rulers were never able to reconquer it. At the beginning of the 11th century, however, the Hungarians accepted Roman Christianity. Their ruler, King Steven I, became the brother-in-law of the German king and invited western European warriors, clerics, miners, merchants, and craftsmen to settle in Hungary. He advised his son to welcome foreigners into his country because they would strengthen his realm.

Similarly, Boleslav I of Poland created a western Christian kingdom that was politically independent of Germany, yet closely associated with it. Very much the same thing happened in Germanic-speaking Denmark at about the same time. Nevertheless, large portions of Baltic Europe remained pagan. In the mid-12th century a northern crusade was launched from Germany against the still-pagan Slavs and Balts who lived between the Elbe and Oder Rivers. This conquest continued along the

Baltic coastline throughout the 13th century until it reached the Gulf of Finland. Military orders such as the Teutonic Knights carved out territories that they ruled themselves.

Economy

Germany became increasingly important economically during the 10th and 11th centuries. Saxony was a place where merchants from the east and the west could meet and trade. Goods and slaves from eastern Europe were exchanged for silver from mines in the Harz Mountains. In the eighth century Saxony had barely been able to produce enough food to feed its own people. In the 11th century, however, it became so productive it was known as "the king's kitchen."

This transformation came about as people cleared and cultivated the broad and fertile plains north of the Harz. The urbanization of Europe, which was taking place in the west, also began to occur in the east. New towns were founded in commercial regions along the shores of the Baltic. These towns usually governed themselves. Their structures of government were generally based on those of Lübeck and Magdeburg.

In the late 13th century the cities of northern Germany formed a confederation called the Hanseatic League to regulate disputes among themselves and to protect their commercial interests in distant countries. Although at the end of the Middle Ages Germany was not developing the centralized governmental institutions of a nation-state, much of Germany enjoyed relatively effective government on a local and regional level.

SEE ALSO
- Charlemagne
- Franks
- Frederick II
- Hanseatic League
- Holy Roman Empire
- Hungary
- Magyars

The German city of Nuremberg in 1493, when it was an important center of trade and manufacturing.

Glass

Glass is a unique material and has long been an important substance. Because it holds liquids and is transparent, it is extremely useful and versatile. These qualities ensured that it was in demand throughout the Middle Ages. It was used as jewelry, in windows, and most importantly, to make beakers, jars, and drinking vessels.

The techniques of glassmaking probably originated in ancient Phoenicia (modern Lebanon). Silica sand was heated to high temperatures to produce molten glass. The glass was then shaped by either pouring it into a mold or by "blowing" it. In this process the glassmaker blew through a long metal tube, at the end of which was a lump of glass, heated until it was soft enough to be shaped.

Lost Expertise

The Romans built on this knowledge and developed extremely high-quality glass and exquisite ways of decorating it. However, much of their expertise was lost in western Europe during the early medieval period. Most vessels from this era were made from a bubbly, pale green or brown glass known as forest glass and were of an extremely low quality.

The most impressive examples of western European medieval glasswork to survive are the stained-glass windows that began to appear in cathedrals in the early 11th century. These windows took the form of mosaics made up of hundreds of individual pieces of colored glass. The windows usually depicted stories from the Bible or episodes from the lives of saints. Generally, however, glass windows were rare in the Middle Ages. First, glass was extremely expensive to make. Second, medieval glassmakers did not have the technical knowledge needed to make large, clear panes of glass.

A sherbet jar made in Persia in the 13th century. The jar is covered by a coating known as a glaze. The glaze gives the vessel its color and shiny appearance.

MURANO

Murano has long been the center of Venice's glassmaking industry. This small island lies to the north of the main part of the city and is about an hour away by rowboat. It became the home of the Venetian glassmakers because the city authorities wanted to remove the risk of fire that was created by their furnaces. In 1291 the authorities therefore decreed that the glassmakers should move away from the main city to Murano.

Here the glassmakers thrived, their work regulated by strict codes and a highly organized guild system. Because the glassmakers played an important part in Venice's economy, they were granted special privileges not enjoyed by other citizens—which included being allowed to wear a sword. The glassmakers of Murano led the world in glass production from the 15th century to the 18th century, when the French emperor Napoleon invaded and disbanded many of the glass houses that had been set up five centuries earlier.

A marriage cup made by the Barovier family of Murano glassmakers in 1445. The Baroviers moved to Murano in 1291 and have been producing glassware ever since. They are the world's oldest family of glassmakers.

The finest glass vessels of the Middle Ages were produced in the countries of the Islamic world. Craftsmen in Egypt, Iran, and Syria developed Roman techniques to create luxury objects of breathtaking beauty. They perfected the art of cutting decoration into glass objects. One of the most famous examples is the Corning Ewer, a glass pitcher that originated in Persia in the late 10th or early 11th century. It was made by covering a colorless glass vessel with a layer of green glass, most of which was then cut away to create an elegant design of stylized animals. This type of glass is known as cameo glass.

Islamic glassmakers also discovered a process of decoration known as luster, probably some time in the eighth century. By applying metallic pigments and firing them using a special process, they found that they could create a beautiful and highly colorful finish. A little later, around the 13th and 14th centuries, they also perfected the art of decorating their glass with gold and brightly colored enamels. Such objects were highly valued and were exported far afield to China and Europe.

However, by the 15th century the center of glass production switched from the Islamic countries to Venice, a trading city then at the height of its prosperity. The Venetians came to dominate glass production for centuries and still make glass today.

SEE ALSO

♦ Cathedrals
♦ House and Home
♦ Mosaic
♦ Venice

GOVERNMENT

A 15th-century illustration showing Richard II of England (1367–1400) surrounded by his royal council. Richard ascended to the English throne when he was only 10 years old—for the first years of his reign his councillors effectively ruled the country.

There was no single dominant type of government in medieval Europe. Depending on when and where they lived, people were governed by local lords, kings, the church, or national or city assemblies. However, toward the end of the medieval period distinct nation-states began to emerge.

In the early Middle Ages most people owed their allegiance to their local lord. Kings and emperors, to whom the lords themselves owed their allegiance, occupied a background role, as did the pope. It was the regional lords who administered justice, levied taxes, and raised armies. But gradually, in parts of Europe such as France and England the king's authority began to grow. The power invested in the king, symbolized by his anointing and coronation, began to take on an aura of religious mystery.

In the early Middle Ages the king was surrounded by bishops and nobles, who were generally in constant competition with one another. They were not always under the monarch's control, especially if he lacked the military power to impose his will on them. On occasion nobles were able to force kings to issue decrees. One example of this type of pressure was the Magna Carta, granted by King John of England in 1215. It protected the nobles, the church, and other free landholders from royal demands.

35

A SENSE OF NATIONHOOD

A number of national monarchies began to emerge in Europe in the late Middle Ages in Scandinavia, eastern Europe, and most importantly, in England and France. While in the early Middle Ages loyalties and a sense of identity were entirely local, by the 14th century a definite distinction was emerging between those born inside and outside the realm.

This distinction was reinforced in several ways. In many countries the cult of the national patron saint, such as England's Saint George, began to gain widespread popular appeal. National heroes, often mythological figures such as King Arthur (more or less invented in the 12th century), were also important in that they engaged people's emotions and loyalties. Above all, the growth in many countries of national literature, written in the mother tongue—be it English, Spanish, French, or Italian—unified peoples' sense of themselves.

A 12th-century mosaic showing King Arthur. Tales of national heroes such as Arthur helped bind nations together.

This relationship began to change, however. The king governed with the help of paid bureaucrats, many of them graduates of the newly formed universities. These civil servants were responsible for administering the law, raising taxes, managing the royal finances, and advising the monarch. Power became far more centralized.

CENTRAL GOVERNMENT

In the earlier Middle Ages kings moved from place to place with their courtiers. In the 13th and 14th centuries, as the new institutions of government became more complex, they began to settle in one place. Royal capitals, such as Paris and London, began to emerge.

In order to curb the power of the nobles, kings began to call into being national assemblies—gatherings of subjects that included the three "estates," or social categories. They were the clergy, the nobility, and the bourgeoisie (the newly emerging middle classes). The role of these national assemblies was to authorize the king's actions, in particular the raising of taxes, and to provide support for the king.

In addition assemblies allowed the voices of the king's subjects to be heard, providing an important counterbalance to the power of the nobility. Gradually, however, the assemblies began to assert their own rights and privileges. For example, in

GOVERNMENT

GOVERNMENT IN SUNG CHINA

In the late 10th century the vast Sung Empire embraced an area seven times the size of modern France, divided, for the purposes of government, into provinces and prefectures that were run by imperial commissioners. General government policy was the responsibility of a council of state consisting of five to nine members and chaired by the emperor. The Sung administration was divided into three departments, which dealt with the economy and finance, the armies, and the administration of justice.

In the 11th century a minister called Wang An-shih (1021–1086) was appointed to reform Sung government. He lightened the burden of peasant farmers by introducing price controls, setting up a system of state loans, and reducing taxes. He also introduced substantial increases in the salaries of state officials and improved the system of recruiting civil servants by introducing examinations on practical subjects. In this way he hoped that the Sung government would be run by public servants who were devoted to the public good.

France the Grand Ordinance of 1357 asserted that the monarch could not levy any taxes without the agreement of the Estates (assembly).

CITIES AND CITY-STATES

While new nations were beginning to emerge, much of Europe was still divided into a patchwork of city-states, dukedoms, clerical states (ruled by bishops), and principalities. For example, the Holy Roman Empire, which covered most of central Europe, was rarely governed by the emperor in the modern sense. Instead, local dukes and princes held power in their own lands. From the 14th century onward trading towns became increasingly independent as well, with their own governing bodies drawn from the merchant classes.

Powerful independent city-states were also common in Italy. In cities such as Milan, Genoa, Florence, and Siena townspeople had begun to assert their rights to govern themselves as early as the 11th and 12th centuries. These governments developed their own systems of taxation, regulated every aspect of urban life, and managed large programs of public works. By the 15th century the city-states of Florence and Milan and the republic of Venice were the major powers in northern Italy. Venice was seen as a model of political stability, with an elected government and a formal head of state, the doge, who was appointed for life.

A portrait of the 15th-century Venetian doge Giovanni Mocenigo. The doge, or leader, was chosen from among the city's leading families. Doges ruled Venice from the eighth to the 18th centuries.

SEE ALSO

- China
- City-states
- England
- Feudalism
- France
- Holy Roman Empire
- Italy
- Parliaments
- Political Thought
- Taxation and Tithes

GRANADA

During the Middle Ages the region of Granada in southern Spain was an Islamic kingdom. It was a flourishing commercial and artistic center, as well as the last stronghold of the Moors to fall to the Christian reconquest. It is also famous as the location of the Alhambra Palace, one of the great masterpieces of medieval Islamic architecture.

The Moors were Arabs, Berbers, and other Muslim peoples from northern Africa, and they first invaded Spain in the early 700s. Under the leadership of the Damascan prince Abd ar-Rahman (ruled 756–788) they created a unified Muslim state. It was known as Andalusia. The state covered much of southern Spain and endured for over 200 years.

By the end of the 10th century, however, different groups of Moors were fighting against each other, and their territory across the Iberian Peninsula split into smaller states. The Zirid dynasty of Berbers took over the Granada region in 972 and ruled there until 1152, when they were overthrown by the Almohads, a tribe from Morocco that practiced an extremely strict form of Islam. The Almohads suffered defeat at the hands of the Christians further north early in the 13th century, and in Granada a new Muslim dynasty came to power—the Nasrids.

THE HILL OF STRANGERS

The Nasrid dynasty ruled Granada from 1238. In Arabic they called their kingdom Gharnata, meaning "hill of strangers." The first Nasrid ruler, Muhammad I, paid tribute to the Christian king Ferdinand III of Castile, a kingdom which bordered on his territory. Muhammad welcomed Muslim refugees from other parts of Spain and began building the famous Alhambra citadel above the growing city of Granada.

These elaborately decorated arches look out onto one of the Alhambra's many courtyards.

GRANADA

Culture in Granada reached its height during the reign of Muhammad V (ruled 1354–1391). Muhammad appointed some of the most learned men of his time as ministers, including scholars, poets, and physicians. He also appointed a special "frontier judge," whose job was to listen to Christian complaints against the Nasrids. This was especially important now that Castile had taken over the Strait of Gibraltar, at the entrance of the Mediterranean, which reduced the power of the Nasrid ports. From 1407 Castile began to plan to invade the kingdom of Granada in order to complete the Christian reconquest of Spain.

The Reconquest

The leading families of Granada, under pressure from the threatening Christians, began to split apart. Some agreed to help the Christian army under Ferdinand the Catholic, and this caused civil war. The Christians seized the port of Malaga and soon laid siege to the city of Granada.

The siege divided the Muslim citizens. Some wanted to give in peacefully, while others were determined to fight the Christians. However, there was no stopping the reconquering forces, and on January 2, 1492, the last Nasrid ruler, Muhammad XI, surrendered his citadel, his city, and his kingdom. So ended Muslim rule in Spain.

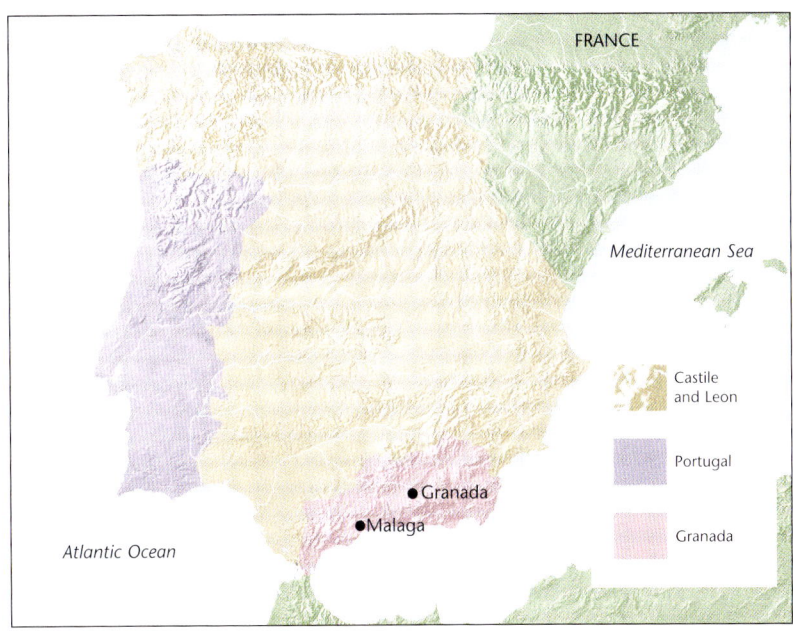

This map shows the extent of the kingdom of Granada at its height in the 14th century.

THE ALHAMBRA

Around 1240 the Nasrids built a fortress on the remains of an ancient stronghold called Alacazaba. They strengthened it with high walls, towers, and ramparts, and called the new citadel Al-Qal'a al-Hambra, which means "the red fort" and refers to the color of its sun-dried bricks. The citadel had offices, houses, shops, mosques, a royal mint, a prison, public baths, and a hospital. It was guarded by a garrison of soldiers.

During the reign of Yusuf I (ruled 1333–1354) the Alhambra was developed into a beautiful palace, with sunny courtyards surrounded by shady arcades and terraces. The gardens, with their fountains and scented plants, made the palace light and cool. Yusuf received foreign visitors in a grand reception room overlooking a beautiful courtyard. Parts of the Alhambra were ruined in the final struggle between the Moors and the Christians. However, much of the original medieval palace has been restored in recent years.

SEE ALSO

♦ Islamic Empire
♦ Spanish Kingdoms

GREAT SCHISM

The Great Schism that lasted from 1378 to 1417 is also known as the Great Western Schism or the Avignon Schism. It was a division in the Roman Catholic church during which there were two rival popes. One pope lived in the French city of Avignon and the other in Rome.

This gold coin bears a portrait of Pope Clement VII. It was the election of Clement in the place of Urban VI that sparked the Great Schism.

In 1309 Pope Clement V (1260–1314) moved the seat of the papacy from Rome to Avignon in France. Clement was closely associated with the French king Philip IV, who had helped ensure his appointment. Clement moved to Avignon partially to avoid the political violence of Italy and partially to be nearer his political ally. For the next 68 years popes ruled from Avignon.

In 1377 Pope Gregory XI returned to Rome, hoping to reunite the western and eastern churches. He died the following year, however, and the college of cardinals elected Urban VI (pope 1378–1389) as his successor. During the following months Urban made attempts to reassert the supreme position of the pope and attacked the wealth and corruption of the church.

Urban's actions offended many of the cardinals who had elected him. A group of them moved back to Avignon. They declared his election invalid, saying that they had been intimidated into voting for him, and elected another pope, Clement VII (pope 1378–1394). Urban, meanwhile, appointed a new college of cardinals. There were now two popes and two sets of cardinals. This split had serious implications for the idea that the pope was God's sole representative on earth. If there were two popes, which one of them was legitimate?

POLITICAL EFFECTS

The schism in the church also affected the political scene because European governments chose sides and were about evenly divided. Supporting Urban VI and Rome were the Holy Roman Empire, Naples, England, and Hungary. Those who favored Clement VII and Avignon were Castile, Aragon, Scotland, and the duchies along the Rhine River. France was divided, the king supporting

GREAT SCHISM

Avignon and the powerful University of Paris supporting Rome. The Roman popes who ruled during the Schism were Urban VI, Boniface IX (pope 1389–1404), Innocent VII (pope 1404–1406), and Gregory XII (pope 1406–1415). The Avignonese popes were Clement VII and Benedict XIII (pope 1394–1417).

The Council of Pisa

In 1407 Gregory XII and Benedict XIII agreed to meet at a town in northern Italy in order to end the schism. For seven months the popes put off meeting one another. The cardinals grew increasingly angry and called for a council to be held at Pisa. Each pope also called for a council in separate locations. Almost no one attended the councils convened by the popes, while the council at Pisa (1409) attracted an assortment of about a thousand cardinals, bishops, abbots, ambassadors, and princes.

The council deposed both popes on the grounds of heresy and elected Alexander V in their place. Since Gregory XII and Benedict XIII refused to leave office, there were now three popes. Even the death of Alexander the next year did not solve anything, because John XXIII was promptly elected in his place.

Under pressure from the Holy Roman emperor John called for another council. He expected his own power to be confirmed. The council was convened in Constance in 1414. It instructed all three popes to abdicate. John refused and fled in disguise, believing that in his absence the council would be forced to disband. Instead, the council placed itself above the authority of the pope. It deposed and ordered the arrest of John, who was imprisoned. Gregory agreed to resign, while Benedict found himself isolated. The council then elected Martin V (1417–1431), who ruled in Rome as the one true pope. At last the schism was over.

The papal palace at Avignon was built between 1334 and 1352. It was home to all the Avignon popes during the years of the Great Schism.

SEE ALSO

- Church
- France
- Heresy
- Papacy
- Roman Catholic Church

THE COUNCIL OF CONSTANCE

The Council of Constance, in session from 1414 to 1418, was a turning point in church history. Pope John XXIII assumed that he would be able to control all decisions because a majority of bishops, who traditionally held the right to vote, supported him. However, it was quickly decided to group the delegates into four "nations"—English, French, German, and Italian—each with an equal vote, no matter how large or small their delegation. Although he had the support of the Italians, John was outvoted when the council gained control over the papacy. This control was made official by the decree *Sacrosancta*, which stated that a general council of the church had authority over the pope.

GREECE

The history of Greece in the Middle Ages was dominated by disasters, including plagues, earthquakes, and a series of invasions. However, these events were separated by periods of prosperity and comparative tranquillity.

Greece had become part of the Roman Empire in 146 B.C. Following the split between Roman west and Byzantine east, Greece was absorbed into the Byzantine Empire. During the rule of the Emperor Justinian (483–565 A.D.) attempts were made to promote Roman law and reduce the level of Greek self-government.

This period was followed by a time when Greece was beset by earthquakes, plagues, and Slavonic invasions from the north. However, by the seventh century the Greeks had found a new national identity through the Orthodox church, which upheld national customs and the Greek language, and opposed interference in Greek affairs from the Byzantine capital, Constantinople.

The Greeks became the major maritime traders in the eastern Mediterranean, and a period of prosperity followed. However, it was interrupted by occasional raids and attacks from western Europe. In 1084 Sicilian Normans gained a foothold on the Ionian islands. In 1146 they sacked the cities of Thebes and Corinth. The expanding Venetian republic, jealous of Greece's dominance of eastern Mediterranean trade, also began to encroach from the 11th century onward.

THE LATIN EMPIRE

In 1204 northern European Crusaders sacked Constantinople, bringing about the temporary end of the Byzantine Empire. All of Greece was subjected to foreign occupation, with the exception of Epirus in the northwest, which was ruled by Michael Angelus, a Byzantine prince. The rest of the country was divided between Frankish barons, Venetians, and Italian adventurers.

The island of Methoni, like much of Greece, was occupied by a variety of different peoples during the Middle Ages. The fortress on the right was built by the Venetians in the 13th century; the tower on the left was added later by the Turks.

GREECE

ATHOS

SEE ALSO
- Byzantine Empire
- Crusades
- Monasteries
- Orthodox Church
- Turkic Peoples

In 885 Emperor Basil I recognized the "Holy Mountain" of Athos, a rocky peninsula situated off Greece's northeastern mainland, as a territory reserved for monks and hermits. Everyone else was banned from Athos—women are still not allowed to visit. The first monastery, the Great Laura, was founded in 963; a further 19 great monasteries were built there between the 10th and 16th centuries.

In most monasteries monks lived, ate, and worked together. Each monastery was linked to a network of outlying farms, chapels, and places for retreat and private prayer. At the tip of the peninsula the retreat of Karoulia provided an ultimate sanctuary for hermits.

Each of the conquerors brought their own language and culture to their new territories. While they allowed natives to retain their own laws and systems of internal administration, the Greek church was brought under the control of Rome, and leading churchmen were exiled.

THE BYZANTINE DECLINE

In 1261 the Byzantines reconquered Constantinople and reinstated an empire that consisted of a network of small states ruled over by descendants of former imperial families. Thessalonica (modern Thessaloniki) was the second most important Byzantine city. The Peloponnesian Peninsula and Thessaly were eventually restored to Byzantine rule. Central Greece was ruled by Burgundians, then occupied by Spanish mercenaries, and eventually occupied by Florentines, when the region enjoyed a brief period of stability and prosperity. Northern Greece was conquered by the Serbian tsar, Stephen Dushan.

Areas of Greece reoccupied by Byzantium prospered between the 13th and 15th centuries. A number of fortified towns were established, such as Larissa, Demetrias, Monemvasia, Patras, and Mistra. These towns were clearly segregated; there were areas for foreign traders and quarters for ethnic or religious minorities, such as Jews. As in western Europe, trade guilds also began to emerge.

The Byzantine emperor granted many of the towns statutes of independence—Monemvasia gained independence in 1259, for example. However, this brief period of prosperity ended in the 15th century, when most of Greece became part of the expanding empire of the Ottoman Turks.

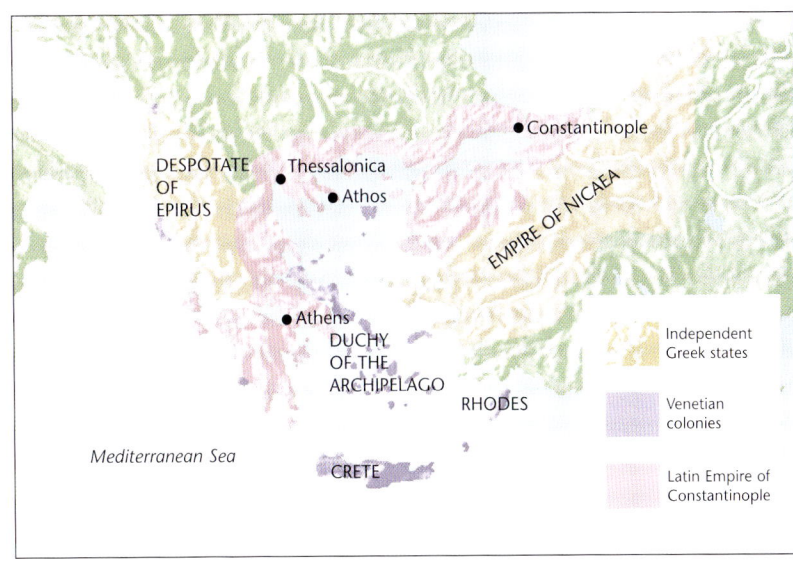

This map of Greece shows those areas that were independent in 1215, as well as those under the control of Venice and the Latin empire of Constantinople.

Gregory the Great

Gregory the Great was born in Rome in about 540 and was pope from 590 until his death in 604. He is known for his work as a monk, politician, pope, and scholar, and is considered to be one of the most important figures in the history of the church.

Gregory was brought up by wealthy Christian parents who made sure that he enjoyed an excellent education. After law school he served as a high government official in Rome. But his desire to serve God prompted him to renounce worldly affairs and turn to the monastic life. He used his family fortune to found a series of monasteries, intending to remain a monk until he died.

However, Italy was in a state of political turmoil since the Lombards, who held all of the north of the country, were threatening to invade Rome. Gregory was sent to Constantinople to try to secure aid against them. Although he failed in this mission, success in other areas demonstrated his abilities, and he was elected pope in 590. Gregory then raised an army and made a truce with the Lombards.

Church Reforms

Within the church Gregory greatly strengthened the position of the pope against that of the patriarch of Constantinople, a rival religious leader. He also reformed the procedure for the election of bishops, brought tribes such as the Franks and Visigoths under the religious control of Rome, and organized successful missionary expeditions to England. He arranged for the church to provide education and welfare for the poor and to supervise the administration of justice.

Gregory was a great scholar and left behind a sizable body of written work, including histories of the church and of the Lombard people. He also made changes in the ritual of mass, contributing to the development of the style of music we now know as Gregorian chant.

An ivory panel from the late 10th century showing Gregory the Great at his writing desk. Gregory wrote many collections of sermons and commentaries on the Bible.

SEE ALSO

- Barbarian Invasions
- Franks
- Music
- Papacy
- Papal States
- Roman Catholic Church

Guilds

Guilds were associations formed by craftsmen, merchants, and other professionals to further the interests of their members. Guilds flourished in Europe from the 11th to the 16th centuries as towns became bigger and more numerous. They played an important part in medieval economic, social, and cultural life.

The coat of arms of the Wool Guild of Florence. In the Middle Ages the guilds wielded huge political power in the city.

The origins of medieval guilds lay in the professional corporations established during the Roman Empire. They had been formed when the state imposed standards for weights and measures and for the quality of work and produce. The Roman government used these corporations to control the distribution and price of food in times of shortage.

Guilds became popular again in 11th- and 12th-century Europe as towns grew big enough to support large numbers of a particular type of merchant or craftsman. These guilds were not state controlled, but instead operated as independent organizations. Associations and clubs were common features of medieval life, and numerous guilds already existed for social and religious purposes. In London in 1125 a knight's guild was formed, and soon the members of many different occupations were forming associations. There was even an association of lepers in London who tried to copy the more fortunate in medieval England by forming themselves into an organized group.

Types of Guilds

In medieval Europe there were two main types of guilds. First, there were the merchant guilds. They were made up of professionals such as doctors, lawyers, and highly skilled artisans like goldsmiths, as well as merchants and money lenders. Merchant guilds were composed of the wealthiest members of medieval towns and cities, and they often exercised considerable political power.

The second type of guild was the craft guild. They were occupational associations that were made up of master craftsmen, such as weavers, stone masons, butchers, and blacksmiths. Even painters and sculptors had their own guilds.

GUILDS AND TOWN LIFE

The practice of concentrating members of a profession in one specific district or on one street led the guilds to become responsible for the organization of civic life in that particular area. The guild activities were centered on the guildhalls, where meetings took place and speeches were made. These occasions were usually marked by lots of ceremonial eating and drinking. Guilds that fined wayward members sometimes even allowed them to pay the penalty in beer. The guilds also adopted patron saints and on feast days and holidays would lead processions and sponsor celebrations in their district. These festivities were also good for business.

The Guildhall at Lavenham, England. As well as being the venues for meetings, guildhalls would often be the main focal point of a town's social life.

In addition to the guilds of master craftsmen there were also societies of journeymen (from the French word *journée*, meaning "a day"). A journeyman was a craftsman who had served his apprenticeship and was qualified to work for any master who would pay him a daily rate. Journeymens' societies pressed employers for wage hikes and sometimes organized strikes.

Frequently, however, journeymens' associations were forbidden and suppressed by the civic authorities, which were themselves composed of the guild-member employers. Sometimes this situation led to riots and rebellions such as the Ciompi rebellion in Florence in 1378. Occasionally, laws were passed that limited the power of the merchant guilds. Generally, however, such guilds enjoyed a great deal of political and economic power. For example, a number of the great Italian city-states—like Florence, Genoa, Siena, and Venice—were governed by a small number of wealthy members of the merchant guilds.

Organizing Trade

The main function of medieval guilds was the organization of local trade. Each guild regulated the prices and quality of goods and the conditions of their production. Each guild was also responsible for training apprentices in their trade or profession and for settling disputes among its members. The guilds' determination to represent the economic interests of their members against all others often led them to establish trade monopolies. This meant that they had exclusive trading rights in their town, and any outside

GUILDS

A section of a stained-glass window in Chartres Cathedral, France, showing a traveling wine merchant. The window was paid for by the wine merchants' guild.

traders—especially foreign ones—were only allowed to trade if they paid heavy tolls.

While guild members were exempt from tolls in their own town, they did have to pay guild fees. The word guild itself comes from the Old English word *gield*, meaning "payment." In exchange guild members also received other benefits related to their guild's vital role in medieval social life. The guilds provided welfare to their members. They looked after sick members and their families, buried their dead, and helped support widows and orphans.

Just as individuals could join together to form a guild, groups of towns could form associations to promote and protect their common interests. By far the most effective association of this type was the Hanseatic League, a group of cities in northern Germany and the Baltic that dominated northern European trade and politics in the 14th century.

GUILDS AND THE ARTS

In addition to their commercial and social enterprises the guilds in medieval Europe played an extremely active role in cultural life. For many guilds an important part of their social presence in the town was to build a chapel or to commission religious paintings and sculptures.

In 1366 in Florence, Italy, the guilds were responsible for building the church and granary of Or San Michele. On the exterior walls of the church are 14 statues representing the patron saints of the guilds that paid for them. Among the most famous statues are those carved by the sculptor Donatello (about 1386–1466), who made the figures of Saint Peter for the butchers' guild, Saint Mark for the weavers, and Saint George for the armorers. Other famous sculptors who made statues for the church include Lorenzo Ghiberti and Nanni di Banco.

A carving from Or San Michele showing stonemasons.

Like medieval society itself, the guild was a hierarchy. It was based on the apprentice system. This system ensured the continuity of practice, tradition, and personnel on which the welfare of the guilds and their members depended.

JOURNEYMEN

Guild membership was reserved for masters. They were established craftsmen of recognized skills who owned and ran their own premises, known as "workshops." A journeyman who could provide proof to the guild of technical competence in the form of a "masterpiece" could then be admitted to the guild and become a master himself, set up his own workshop, and train his own apprentices.

Apprentices formed the lowest level of the medieval guild structure. They were often as young as eight years old and lodged in the master's house and received their food, clothing, and education in the trade. In return, apprentices worked without payment for a period set by the guild. Apprenticeships were extremely valued and sought after, and in some cases were awarded only to members of the master's own family, a system that caused widespread resentment.

Depending on the type of trade or profession, an apprentice could be training for up to seven years. Traces of this medieval practice are still evident today in the length of training for certain professions such as doctors and lawyers. After completing his training to guild standards, an apprentice could leave the master and work independently as a journeyman. Alternatively, he could stay with his master and become his assistant.

SEE ALSO

- Children
- Education
- Fairs and Markets
- Hanseatic League
- Manufacturing
- Painting and Sculpture
- Trade

Hanseatic League

The Hanseatic League, or Hansa, was a confederation of trading towns, most of which were in northern Germany. The Hansa towns joined with German merchants throughout northern Europe to protect their trade. Their league flourished from the 14th to the 16th century.

Early in the 13th century the Baltic port of Lübeck became an important town for Saxon merchants who wanted to trade with eastern Europe. Visby, further north on the Swedish island of Gotland, was the main port for trade with Novgorod and Russia. The Baltic sea route between Lübeck and Visby was a busy one, and German merchants came to dominate the whole of the Baltic region.

At the same time, far to the south in Cologne on the Rhine River, merchants had made agreements with cities such as Bruges and London to help trade with Flanders and England. In the 1270s an association of merchants around Lübeck and Hamburg joined together with the Rhinelanders to trade jointly, and a few years later the other Baltic ports did the same. This was the beginning of the Hanseatic League.

The twin towers of St. Mary's Church in Lübeck. The church was built in the 12th and 13th centuries.

Protection in Numbers

The name for the league comes from the Old German word *hanse*, meaning "company." German merchants were used to forming small versions of these companies in order to help each other against robbers on land and pirates at sea. The Hanseatic League simply joined all the smaller associations together.

Member towns and cities helped each other establish trading bases and then controlled trade by winning special privileges and then creating monopolies so that no one else could compete with them. The league gave gifts and loans to the leaders of foreign towns; but if these did not bring the favors they were seeking,

MEDIEVAL WORLD

A map showing the most important members of the Hanseatic League. The towns' location near the Baltic Sea meant that they could deal in raw materials from Russia and Finland and manufactured goods from England and Flanders.

they sometimes threatened to stop trade and cut off that particular town. In extreme cases the league even used armed force to get its way.

The league was governed by a congress of merchants that met occasionally, usually at Lübeck. If a town refused to join the league, its merchants soon found that they could not sell their goods in the right markets. The league traded mainly in furs and timber from Russia, wool from Flanders, and fish from Norway and Sweden. By the 14th century there were at least 100 member towns, each of which had its own office where merchants could trade goods and information. The towns defended their independence from local nobles and regional rulers.

During the 15th century the league began to lose its power as neighboring regions increased their trade. The Netherlands and England became powerful in northern Europe, and Sweden became important in the Baltic Sea. The Hanseatic League held its last assembly in 1669.

SEE ALSO

♦ City-states
♦ Germany
♦ Guilds
♦ Trade

LÜBECK

The medieval port of Lübeck is located near the mouth of the Trave River, where it flows into the Baltic Sea. It was founded in 1143 by Count Adolf II of Holstein and, after burning down, was rebuilt in 1159 by Henry the Lion (about 1130–1185), duke of Bavaria and Saxony. Henry was leading German expansion eastward under the Holy Roman emperor Frederick Barbarossa, and he developed Lübeck into a commercial center.

At the beginning of the 13th century Lübeck was captured by Denmark, but in 1226 it was made a free city. That meant it could govern itself and make its own laws, which set an example for more than 100 other towns in the Baltic region. The Hanseatic League made Lübeck its administrative center in 1358, since it was the main trading port between the regions of eastern Europe and manufacturing towns in the west.

Hapsburgs

The House of Hapsburg was one of Europe's greatest and most famous royal families. The Hapsburgs ruled the Holy Roman Empire from 1273 until 1308 and from 1438 until 1806. They also ruled Austria until 1918.

The Hapsburg family took their name from Habichtsburg, the castle that was their home from the early 11th century. The castle overlooks the Aare River in the northern region of modern Switzerland. By the end of the 11th century the family had gained more lands around Lake Lucerne and was using the title count of Hapsburg. During the 12th century their faithful service to the Hohenstaufen kings, who ruled over the duchy of Swabia, helped increase their power and influence. They soon became one of the most important and powerful families in Germany.

An Unlikely Emperor

The first Hapsburg emperor, Rudolf, was born in 1218. As a young man he was a loyal supporter of the Hohenstaufen Holy Roman emperor Frederick II and his son Conrad IV. Conrad died in 1254, and in the following 19 years three separate families held the imperial throne. Then in 1273 Rudolf was elected emperor. This happened mainly because the nobles who elected the emperor wanted to keep out a non-German rival, Otakar II of Bohemia.

In some ways Rudolf was an unlikely candidate. He was 7 ft. (2.1m) tall and extremely thin, with a small, bald head. He also liked to wear peasant's clothes in an age when nobles and monarchs were always to

This stained glass window shows Rudolf I, the first member of the Hapsburg family to be Holy Roman emperor. The shield held in his left hand bears the symbol of the House of Hapsburg. This eagle appears on the national flag of Austria to this day.

be seen in luxurious garments. In 1274 Pope Gregory X recognized him as emperor, and two years later he defeated Otakar II in battle. He gave the duchies of Austria and Styria to his two sons, starting more than 600 years of Hapsburg rule over Austria. Rudolf died in 1291.

Rudolf I could not persuade the electors to choose his elder son Albert (1255–1308) to succeed him as emperor. They chose Adolf of Nassau instead, but Albert managed to form an alliance with the electors and get rid of Adolf. Albert was then emperor

51

FREDERICK III

Frederick III was elected emperor in 1440, but it was not until 12 years later that he became the last Holy Roman emperor to be crowned by the pope in Rome. Like many Holy Roman emperors, Frederick spent most of his reign engaged in struggles with rival claimants to his throne.

Frederick was famous for his bizarre physical appearance. His jaw and lower lip jutted out markedly from his face, and he passed this characteristic down to his son Maximilian I. Later members of the Hapsburg dynasty tended to marry relations to prevent people from rival families from claiming the throne. This inbreeding led the "Hapsburg lip" to become even more prominent.

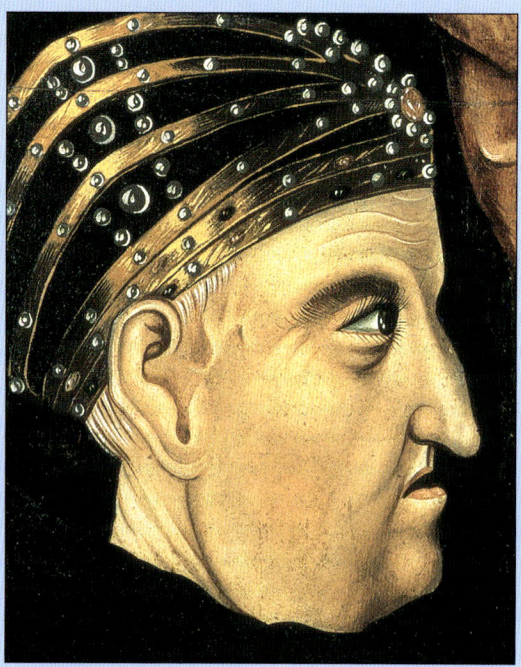

Frederick III was the first Hapsburg monarch to possess the famous "Hapsburg lip," the jutting chin that identified members of the family for years to come.

for 10 years before he was murdered by his nephew, John of Swabia. This meant that the Hapsburgs lost the imperial crown. It would be 130 years before they recaptured it.

During the rest of the 14th century, while other powerful families contested the throne, the Hapsburgs moved their main residence to Vienna and concentrated on increasing their Austrian territories. The new head of the family, Duke Rudolf IV, increased their power in Vienna and had a great impact on the city.

The Hapsburgs eventually regained the imperial throne in 1438. Albert V (1397–1439), who was then head of the house and duke of Austria, married the daughter of the Holy Roman emperor Sigismund. On his father-in-law's death Albert became king of Bohemia and Hungary, and in the following year emperor.

After his death Frederick III (1415–1493), from another branch of the family, became head of the Hapsburg dynasty. In 1477 Frederick arranged for his son Maximilian (1459–1519) to marry Mary of Burgundy. This has been called the most important marriage in European history because it gave the house of Hapsburg territories in the Low Countries and France, and made the Austrians a major European power. Frederick's motto was made up of the five vowels—A.E.I.O.U. They stood for *Austriae est imperare orbi universo*, Latin for "Austria is destined to rule the world."

The Hapsburgs would go on to be Holy Roman emperors for hundreds of years to come, ruling over areas as distant as Sicily and Spain. The last Hapsburg emperor, Francis II, gave up the title in 1806.

SEE ALSO

♦ Germany
♦ Holy Roman Empire

HEAVEN AND HELL

In medieval Europe life expectancy was extremely low. The idea of an afterlife, therefore, was something that played an extremely important part in peoples' lives. The concepts of heaven and hell also provided people with a strong incentive to follow the teachings of the church.

The Last Judgment by the 15th-century German painter Stefan Lochner. On the left of the picture angels guide the righteous into heaven. On the right sinners are tormented by demons in hell.

According to the Bible, heaven is the home of God and his angels and a place of reward for Christian believers after death. Hell is the abode of the devil and his demons, a place of darkness, fire, and everlasting pain prepared for people who have led sinful lives.

The Christian concept of hell was based on the Judaic Gehenna or Gehinnom. This Jewish hell was named after the Valley of Hinnom, a desolate region just south of Jerusalem. Between the 10th and sixth centuries B.C. the Philistines practiced human sacrifice there by burning children in ceremonial fires. Jewish law taught that sinners would burn eternally in similar fires, the origin of the Christian idea of hellfire.

Medieval religious thinkers, writers, and artists were quick to expand on the idea of hell. According to one bishop, the fire of hell burned hot but gave absolutely no light. The religious writer Thomas Aquinas, on the other hand, warned that hellfire gave just enough light to permit the damned to see the horrors around them.

THE ISLAMIC AFTERLIFE

The Muslim understanding of life after death is graphically described in the Koran. First comes Judgment Day, when everyone is resurrected from their graves. Their deeds, good and bad, are weighed in the balances, and the people are separated accordingly. Infidels, or nonbelievers, are sent to hell, a seven-level place of scorching wind and scalding water under black smoke.

Faithful Muslims ascend to Heaven across a wide bridge over the chasm of hell. When infidels attempt to cross the bridge, it shrinks to the width of a razor's edge, and they fall into the flaming chasm. Believers arrive safely in heaven, a cool garden with pure springs of water, shady trees, and silken couches. While most Muslims had to pass through a form of purgatory before reaching this heaven, it was an immediate reward for any Muslim soldier killed in religious warfare.

A 16th-century Persian painting showing the prophet Muhammad ascending to heaven. He is guided by the angel Gabriel, who hovers in front of him.

In his poem *The Divine Comedy* Dante Alighieri (1265–1321) described a journey through hell, where he observed all the greatest sinners in history. The inhabitants of Dante's hell endured a variety of colorful punishments. Some lay face-downward in a tarpit, while others were locked in ice. Corrupt archbishops and nobles could be seen gnawing on each other's necks.

VISIONS OF HEAVEN

In contrast, the church described heaven as a place of light, bliss, and beauty. In the early medieval period it was pictured as a garden full of fragrant roses, lilies, and violets that never fade. It was also a place where peasants never needed to work. The temperature was always moderate, and birds sang in shady groves of trees.

Somewhat after 1200, when European towns began to thrive, it became more common to describe heaven as a glorious city. The gates, walls, and streets of this heavenly city shone in golden splendor, and its inhabitants dressed in fine silk robes. In the middle of the city lived God, Christ, the Virgin Mary, angels, and the holiest saints.

One concept that grew more popular as the Middle Ages went on was that of purgatory. Purgatory was an intermediate place where the souls of repentant sinners resided before they went to heaven. The doctrine was first popularized by Pope Gregory I (about 540–604). In purgatory the souls of the dead suffer for their sins, but go through a period of purification that allows them eventually to enter heaven.

SEE ALSO

♦ Black Death
♦ Dante
♦ Death and Burial
♦ Islam
♦ Miracles and Mysticism
♦ Thomas Aquinas

HERALDRY

Heraldry was a system of visual symbols that developed in the Middle Ages. It allowed powerful individuals to identify themselves and their possessions and to advertise their ancestry. The system became so complex that heralds were used to oversee a person's right to bear such identification.

Heraldry began in western Europe during the 12th century as a means to identify a lord or knight in battle or during tournaments, when they were totally covered in armor. Without some form of badge they could not easily be identified, either by friend or foe. Emblems first appeared on shields, but were later added to surcoats, the long sleeveless tunics that soldiers wore over their armor. The badges became known as coats of arms, or simply arms.

A 14th-century stained-glass window from Tewkesbury Abbey, England, showing four noblemen in full armor. Each wears his coat of arms on his surcoat.

The fashion for wearing arms spread throughout Europe, and some organization was needed to prevent duplication. Heralds, messengers of the great lords, created a system that became known as heraldry. They controlled the allocation of arms and the form they took. Heralds developed their own special language known as blazon, which used mainly French words. Blazon allowed heralds to make written or spoken descriptions of arms.

COLORS IN HERALDRY

Five basic colors were used in heraldry—azure (blue), gules (red), purpure (purple), sable (black), and vert (green). There were also metallic colors. The metals were or (gold) and argent (silver), although they were usually represented as yellow and white respectively. Colors and metals were called tinctures. Symbols, known as charges, could appear on the field (surface) of a shield or surcoat. They fell into three groups—shapes, plants and animals, and handmade objects.

Shapes included circles with large open centers (annulets), broad diagonal bands (bends), five-pointed stars (mullets), and crosses (saltires). The words dexter and sinister were used to describe the right- and left-hand sides of the shield respectively. A bend sinister, therefore, would be a

55

diagonal stripe that went from the top left of the shield to the bottom right, from the wearer's viewpoint.

Animals, both real and imaginary, were also common. They included eagles, lions, and wild boars. Popular mythical beasts were dragons and unicorns. Animals could be shown in a variety of ways, and special terms developed to describe these poses. Passant animals walked naturally, while rampant animals reared upright with their hind legs on the ground. Animals were also pictured dormant (sleeping), combattant (fighting), and sejant (sitting). Plants found in heraldry included the fleur-de-lys (a stylized lily) and the oak leaf. Popular handmade devices included axes, castles, and ships.

Family Arms

People would pass down coats of arms on a hereditary basis from generation to generation. Noblemen would often incorporate the emblems of their wife's family into their own coat of arms. Because of this arms became increasingly complex, with shields often subdivided into many different sections, each representing a different aspect of family history.

This 14th-century book illustration shows two knights jousting in a tournament. The coats of arms on their shields and their horses' coats allow spectators to identify them.

Heraldic designs are still created. In England the College of Arms will devise arms for an individual, town or city, or large business. Many political emblems, such as the Great Seal of the United States, the symbol of the authority of the federal government, are examples of modern heraldry.

SEE ALSO

- Chivalry
- Japan
- Knights
- Nobility
- Tournaments and Jousts

JAPANESE HERALDRY

In Japan, the only center of medieval heraldry outside Europe, the system of rank identification was known as *mon*. *Mon* developed in the 12th century and was used by great lords and their families. Designs first appeared on clothing and on canopied carts. By the end of the 13th century heraldic devices were also displayed on the shields and armor of the samurai (knights). A system of regulation gradually evolved by the 16th century that permitted samurai to wear their emblems twice on the upper chest, on both sleeves, and on the back.

Heraldic devices used in Japan were even more varied than in Europe. They could include not only animals, such as the crane and the lobster, and mythical beasts, such as the phoenix, but also written characters—which never appeared in European heraldry.

HERESY

The word "heresy" literally means "wrong belief." It is far more important in the history of Christianity than in other world religions because, since Saint Paul, Christianity has been a set of beliefs about God and the relation of Jesus to God. Judaism and Islam, in contrast, are religions of law and practices governing daily life and worship.

As Greeks and Romans converted to Christianity in the early centuries A.D., the intellectuals among them tried to understand the meaning of the divine nature of God, the Holy Spirit, and Jesus Christ. This led to many complicated debates among churchmen. When one side in these debates became predominant or was approved by a church council, the other side was declared heretical.

This statue of Jan Hus is on the Charles Bridge in Prague in the Czech Republic. Hus's criticisms of the pope and the church in Rome led to his being burned as a heretic.

ARIANISM

One dispute centered on the ideas of the Alexandrian priest Arius (about 250–336), who said that the divinity of Jesus could not be the same as the divinity of God, but only similar to it. To settle the dispute, the emperor Constantine summoned a council to Nicaea in 325. This council composed a statement of beliefs opposing the views of Arius. However, before the council met, missionaries had gone off to convert a Germanic tribe called the Goths to Christianity. The missionaries were followers of Arius, so the Goths became "Arian" Christians, heretics in the eyes of the orthodox church.

HUNTING OUT HERETICS

It was not until the 12th century that the Roman church began to actively seek out and punish heretics. Before then bishops had excommunicated those who advocated wrong beliefs or imprisoned them in monasteries. A few were lynched by mobs. The spread of the Cathars and other heresies brought demands from the church that nobles punish heretics caught in their lands.

In 1184 Pope Lucius III organized the special procedure of inquisition to stamp out false belief. Specially trained inquisitors (investigators) were given the task of seeking out heretics, rather than waiting for them to be brought to the attention of church officials. In the 13th century the procedure became increasingly brutal, and in 1252 pope Innocent IV authorized the use of torture to extract confessions from suspected heretics. Those who refused to return to the "true" faith could be burned at the stake in a public ceremony known by the Spanish term *auto-da-fé* (act of faith).

The Pelagians were another group of ancient heretics. They believed that all humans had the free will to live a life without sin. This view ran contrary to the dominant belief that human beings were born as sinners and were dependent on the grace of God to deliver them to salvation.

THE CATHARS

One of the most important heretical groups to emerge in the 12th century were the Cathars. The name "Cathar" comes from a Greek word meaning "pure." They believed there were two gods, one good and one evil. The good god had created the world of spiritual beings, and the evil god had created the material world. Those who practiced the strictest form of Catharism were known as "Perfects." They ate no meat, eggs, or milk and refrained from sexual intercourse.

The Cathars developed from various groups who lived in the Balkans. They were Christians whose ideas were influenced by Manicheanism or other forms of belief in two gods. Missionaries came from the Balkans to western Europe. In the 12th century groups of Cathars appeared in Italy, Germany, and western and southern France.

The Cathars were caught up in regional and church politics when an envoy of Pope Innocent III was murdered by agents of the count of Toulouse in 1208. Innocent accused the count of protecting heretics and called for a crusade against both the count and the Cathars. Crusaders came from all over northern Europe, and the warfare lasted for nearly 20 years. It was at this time that the Cathars came to be known as "Albigensians" after the town of Albi in southern France. Though the region was conquered and inquisitors were very active, the Cathars remained in this region and in Italy and northern Spain for at least another 100 years.

The Waldensians were another important group of heretics. The movement was founded by a former merchant called Peter Waldo (died

HERESY

A contemporary painting of the execution of the 15th-century Italian preacher Girolamo Savonarola. The Dominican was an enemy of Pope Alexander VI, and his accusations of papal corruption led to his being burned as a heretic.

about 1216). In 1175 Waldo adopted a vow of poverty and began to preach the Bible. He soon attracted a following of illiterate men and women called the Poor Men of Lyons, all of whom began to preach. Wearing simple woolen garments, they went out in pairs and spread the Gospel throughout Europe.

TRANSLATING THE BIBLE

One of the most important features of the Waldensians was that they used translated versions of the Bible at a time when church scripture was in Latin. They also believed that the Bible was the final authority in all matters of doctrine, not the pope, and that all Christians were equal before God. In 1184 Pope Lucius III (pope 1181–1185) declared that the Waldensians were heretics.

After this date the Waldensians began to attack what they believed to be the corrupt nature of the Catholic church. They rejected key Catholic doctrines such as the concept of purgatory, the place where the souls of the dead reside before passing to heaven or hell.

From the early 13th century onward there were repeated attempts to wipe out the Waldensians. In 1211 at the French city of Strasburg 80 Waldensians were burned alive. The Roman Catholic crusade against the Albigensians in France was also directed at the Waldensians, many of whom were killed. Persecution continued, and by the end of the 15th century the group was confined to the French and Italian Alps.

Another group who attacked the wealth and worldliness of the church

59

JOHN WYCLIFFE

John Wycliffe (about 1329–1384) was a professor of religious studies at the University of Oxford in England. He opposed the church on many doctrines and practices, especially that of using only Latin for religious services. He also attacked what he saw as the excessive wealth of the church. These beliefs greatly angered the authorities in Rome. In 1377 Pope Gregory XI called for his arrest.

Wycliffe, however, was protected by John of Gaunt, duke of Lancaster. Like Wycliffe, John was concerned about the power of the church, though for more selfish reasons. Wycliffe continued to question the authority of the pope and helped organize the first full English translation of the Bible. Wycliffe died a natural death, but the Council of Constance (1414–1418) declared his teachings heretical and ordered that his bones be dug up and burned.

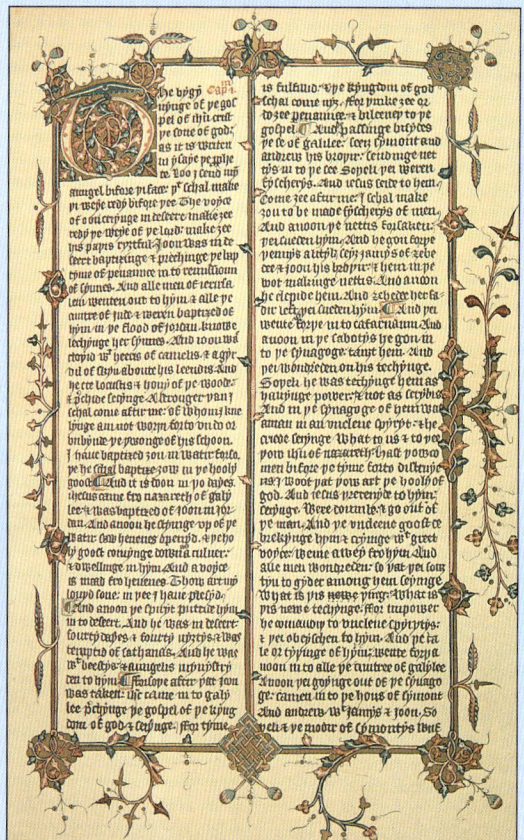

A page from the Wycliffe Bible, the first full English translation of the scriptures. Previously, the Bible had always been written in Latin. The translation allowed many people to read the scriptures for themselves for the first time.

and the authority of Rome were the Hussites. They were followers of the highly respected Czech preacher Jan Hus (1373–1415), himself influenced by the English heretic John Wycliffe.

In his sermons Hus denounced what he saw as the evils in the church, in particular its centralization in Rome and the doctrine of papal sovereignty. He said that Christ alone was the foundation of the church, not Saint Peter and his successors in Rome. Hus refused to agree with the condemnation of Wycliffe and continued to preach the need to reform the Czech church.

In 1414 Hus was summoned to the Council of Constance to defend his views. The Holy Roman emperor promised to guarantee his safety, but Hus was arrested, imprisoned, and burned at the stake the following year.

Many of Hus's followers became caught up in a movement for Bohemian independence. Others insisted that all faithful Christians should be given consecrated wine at the Mass and not just priests. When they were excluded from Catholic congregations, they formed their own churches. Attacked by crusading armies, they were finally defeated in 1434. After the Council of Basel agreed to their demand to receive the consecrated wine, they were readmitted to the Catholic church.

SEE ALSO

- Hus, Jan
- Inquisition
- Roman Catholic Church

HILDEGARD OF BINGEN

Hildegard of Bingen was a German nun and visionary. Her contributions to medieval literature, science, and music made her one of the most influential figures of her time.

Hildegard was born in 1098, the tenth child of a noble family. When she was 14, she entered the Benedictine monastery at Disibodenberg, and in 1136 she became its head (abbess). Since early childhood Hildegard had experienced visions that she interpreted as revelations from God, and in 1141 she was finally persuaded to write them down in a collection called *Scivias* (*Scito vias dominus* or *Know the Ways of the Lord*).

The book brought Hildegard to the attention of the archbishop of Mainz, and in 1148 a committee of church scholars investigated Hildegard's visions and declared them divine. Official acceptance gave Hildegard great authority, and she was soon corresponding with great religious and political leaders like Saint Bernard of Clairvaux and Frederick I Barbarossa.

In 1147 Hildegard established a new convent at Rupertsberg near Bingen, where she wrote two important medical texts. *Physica* (Medicine) and *Causa et curae* (Causes and Cures) demonstrate a powerful imagination and sound scientific observation that were rare in the Middle Ages. In these books Hildegard listed numerous medicinal herbs and drugs, made the connection between sugar and diabetes, and wrote about the relationship between the brain and the nervous system. Hildegard was also a gifted musician and composer.

Following Hildegard's death in 1179, numerous miracles were reported at her tomb. Although she was never officially made a saint, Hildegard is revered as one in some towns in Germany that celebrate her feast day of September 17.

An illustration from Hildegard's *Scivias*, dating from the 12th century. It shows nine choirs of angels, one of her visions.

SEE ALSO

- Medicine
- Miracles and Mysticism
- Music
- Science

MEDIEVAL WORLD

History Writing

During the Middle Ages, especially from the 12th century onward, there was a great explosion of history writing, with subjects ranging from lives of saints to chronicles of war to collections of stories and legends.

An illustration from Jean Froissart's *Chronicles*, showing the Battle of Crécy of 1346. Froissart's book concentrates on the Hundred Years' War between England and France.

Much of the history writing of early medieval Europe was produced by monks. One of the most important of these monastic historians was Saint Bede (about 673–735), an English Benedictine monk who wrote the *Ecclesiastical History of the English Nation*. Another important work on this topic was the *History of the Kings of Britain* (about 1136), a collection of stories from Britain's Celtic past by Geoffrey of Monmouth (died 1154).

It is important not to think of such works as accurate histories in the modern sense. Bede's main goal was to strengthen people's faith in God. His work is thus full of accounts of miracles and visions. Geoffrey of Monmouth's work, meanwhile, was based on myths and legends, and even today historians are unsure as to whether many of the characters in his book really existed.

Histories of War

Chronicles of war were popular in later medieval Europe, and their authors became internationally famous. Jean Froissart (1333–1401) was a Frenchman who traveled freely across national borders to collect information about war. Froissart's accounts are full of praise for chivalric deeds and are highly romanticized.

Many historians were based around the court of the dukes of Burgundy. The works of Philip of Commynes (about 1447–1511) are unique in that they describe conflict from the realistic point of view of a soldier and diplomat. His picture of political intrigues and conspiracies is unusually clear-sighted for the Middle Ages.

The Islamic world also had many chroniclers. The greatest was Ibn Khaldun (1332–1406). He was the first writer to examine the economic forces that shape history. The 20th-century historian A. J. Toynbee described Ibn Khaldun's philosophy of history, *Muqaddimah*, as "the greatest work of its kind that has ever yet been created by any mind."

SEE ALSO

♦ Anglo-Saxons
♦ Islamic Scholarship
♦ Literature

HOLY ROMAN EMPIRE

The Holy Roman Empire was a vast territory that at times included modern-day Germany, Austria, Switzerland, the Czech Republic, eastern France, and parts of Italy. It lasted for over 1,000 years. During this period the relative power of the emperor, pope, and the various regional dukes and princes changed constantly, as did the boundaries of the empire.

Although the term Holy Roman Empire was only used from 1157, the birth of the empire can be dated back to Christmas Day 800, when Pope Leo III crowned Charlemagne (742–814) emperor of the Romans. The pope made this move in order to cement an alliance between the new emperor's powerful Frankish kingdom and the papacy. After Charlemagne's son died in 840, the empire split into three kingdoms ruled by Charlemagne's grandsons.

The title of emperor passed through the hands of various members of Charlemagne's family, but by the late ninth century the holders of the title had little influence. The next really powerful emperor was Otto I (912–973). Pope John XII crowned him emperor of the Romans in 962, after Otto had helped the pope against his enemies in Italy.

ELECTING THE EMPEROR

From this point the title of emperor was held by a German prince or duke. However, the title was not inherited. The emperor was elected by a group of the more important German dukes, kings, and princes, collectively known as the electors. Once he was elected, he was known by the title of German king or king of the Romans. Once crowned by the pope, he could claim the title emperor.

From the late 10th to the middle of the 11th century the balance of power between the emperor and the pope was very much in the favor of the emperor. Rulers such as Henry III (1017–1056) were able to depose popes and effectively decide who their successors were going to be. However, in 1073 the relationship changed dramatically with the election of Pope Gregory VII (about 1020–1085). Gregory was not afraid of confrontation.

Gregory believed that the emperor should be subject to the authority of the pope and not the other way around. A series of disputes with the Holy Roman emperor Henry IV (1050–1106) led to Gregory attempting to depose the emperor and excommunicating him, denying him the right to take part in church rituals.

The crown of the Holy Roman emperor was made for the coronation of Otto I in 962.

MEDIEVAL WORLD

At its height the Holy Roman Empire covered a vast section of central Europe. However, it was rarely united, and many of its regions were effectively independent.

There followed a long period when the pope and emperor were in conflict. The emperors began to distance themselves from Rome. In fact, one of the main reasons why Frederick I (1123–1190) began to describe his territory as the Holy Roman Empire was to separate it from the Holy Church.

The Holy Roman Empire was not just marked by conflicts between the emperor and the pope. There were also constant disputes among the various princes and dukes whose lands made up the empire. After the death of Frederick II in 1250 this conflict was so great that the princes could not decide on a successor until 1273, when Rudolf I (1218–1291) of the Hapsburg family was elected king.

THE HAPSBURGS

Rudolf was the first of a long line of Hapsburg rulers. However, from this point in time the power of the emperor was greatly diminished. Powerful regional rulers like the duke of Saxony were supreme in their own lands. The ties between the empire and the church also grew weaker as the practice of the pope crowning the emperor gradually died out—the last emperor to have a papal coronation was Charles V in 1530. The empire continued to exist in some form or another until 1806, but by this time the title of emperor was almost meaningless.

SEE ALSO

- Charlemagne
- Church
- Frederick I
- Frederick II
- Germany
- Hapsburgs
- Papacy

OTTO III

One of the most ambitious of the early Holy Roman emperors was Otto III (980–1002). Otto was elected German king in 983, when he was just two years old. However, until the age of 14 his guardians ruled for him. In 996 Otto set out for Rome to help Pope John XV put down a rebellion; but by the time he arrived, the pope was dead. Otto succeeded in getting his young cousin Bruno elected as the first German pope. Bruno took the name Gregory V and then promptly crowned Otto emperor.

Unlike most other emperors, Otto was determined to make Rome the capital of his empire. He wanted to revive the glories of ancient Rome, but the young emperor was out of tune with the times. The Roman citizens rebelled against him and besieged his palace. Otto was forced to withdraw to a monastery near Ravenna, where he died at the age of only 21.

64

Horses

The horse played a central role in medieval life. Farmers exploited its strength to pull plows, while in battle mounted warriors were able to take advantage of their speed and maneuverability. Horses were also used for transport and hunting. Gradually, a sizable industry grew up in which people bred, sold, and cared for them.

This illustration from a 14th-century Persian manuscript shows mounted Mongol warriors in battle. The Mongols were the greatest military horsemen in history.

In the Middle Ages a number of technological developments revolutionized the potential of the horse as a working animal. One important step forward was the invention of the modern harness in about 800. This harness ensured that the weight of heavy loads was borne by the horse's powerful shoulders, rather than the neck, which meant that it could be used as a plow animal. Plow horses were able to move much faster than oxen, which had been used previously, allowing fields to be turned over more regularly. This development greatly improved yields.

With the invention of wagon shafts, which attached a wagon to a horse by means of a breastband, or horse collar, horses also began to replace oxen as draft animals. One horse, as opposed to two oxen, could pull a four-wheeled wagon or two-wheeled cart along a bumpy road. They could cover distances much more quickly than oxen and by the 12th century were widely used.

A large industry grew up around the breeding and selling of horses and the making of equipment such as saddles, harnesses, and horseshoes. Horses were traded at special fairs, where a warhorse, known as a destrier, would cost a considerable amount of money. A destrier would fetch several hundred times as much as a simple peasant workhorse, which by the mid-13th century was widely affordable.

Horses in War

The most accomplished military horsemen of the medieval world were the nomads who roamed the Central Asian steppes. From an early age boys spent most of their waking lives in the saddle. They quickly became expert riders. The main weapon used by these nomadic warriors was the bow. The mounted archer was a fearsome foe, and in the early medieval period tribes such as the Huns inflicted a series of crushing military defeats on their western enemies.

The first western people to make effective military use of horses were the Franks in the eighth century. The Franks were famous for their heavy cavalry, armored knights who charged into their enemies in close formation. Key pieces of technology that enabled this development included the stirrup and the war saddle, which was attached to the horse by a single belt. Historians are divided as to exactly when these pieces of equipment were introduced to the West, but agree that they gave the mounted knight far greater stability.

By the 10th and 11th centuries the mounted knight had become one of the most important individuals in the medieval army. The introduction of the stirrup had allowed the knight to develop a new style of fighting, using what was known as a "couched lance." The knight charged at the enemy with the blunt end of his lance tucked underneath his arm and the sharp point sticking horizontally forward. When large numbers of knights charged together in this way, they could prove to be an almost unstoppable force.

A modern farmer using a traditional horsedrawn plow. The development of harnesses such as the one used here allowed medieval farmers to use horses as draft animals

BREEDS OF HORSES

The breeds of horse that were native to western Europe tended to be quite small—today they would be described as ponies. As the knights of Europe began to wear heavier and heavier armor, they required stronger and larger horses. The Islamic conquests of Spain had introduced to Europe new types of horse such as the Barb and the Arabian. By crossbreeding them with native strands, people in the West were able to produce horses of a superior quality.

SEE ALSO

- Agriculture
- Central Asian Peoples
- Franks
- Huns
- Knights
- Mongols
- Tools and Technology
- Transport
- Warfare

HOSPITALS

This 15th-century illustration shows patients in a ward at the Hôtel Dieu in Paris. The lack of space meant that the patients were forced to share beds.

Hospitals existed from the very start of the medieval period. In western Europe they were run almost exclusively by the church. The Christian faith emphasized the importance of looking after one's fellow human beings, and so the church played an active role in the care of the sick.

Many people in medieval Europe lived on the edge of starvation—they were malnourished and extremely vulnerable to illness. Diseases caused by food deficiencies and impure water were widespread, as were infectious illnesses such as smallpox. Some diseases, such as leprosy, were seen as external signs of sin, and lepers, as well as the crippled and maimed, were treated as social outcasts.

The modern concept of the hospital dates to the early fourth century, when Saint Basil of Caesarea built a hospital in Cappadocia, in modern Turkey. Religious institutions within the Eastern Roman Empire gradually began to found similar hospitals, which were originally buildings that housed not only the sick, but also the poor and elderly. Monastic infirmaries then began to spread throughout the west. The Hôtel Dieu of Lyon, France, was founded in 542, and the Hôtel Dieu of Paris in 660. Medical treatment was extremely limited, but the monks who ran the hospitals did have some knowledge of herbal remedies, and grew medicinal herbs in the hospital gardens.

Religious institutions continued to play a major part in the development of hospitals. The Benedictine order alone is said to have founded 2,000 hospitals. During the Crusades the growth of hospitals accelerated, and military hospitals began to appear along main Crusader routes.

The Knights Hospitalers of the Order of St. John founded a hospital in Jerusalem that could treat 2,000 patients. It was famous for its treatment of eye disease, and operations to cure cataracts were performed there. Most operations, however, were crude. Surgeons used butchers' implements, and amputation was common. The only anesthetics available were alcohol and opium, and patients often died during the course of operations.

Hospitals were mainly for the poor or those far from home. Most sick or injured people were cared for at their own houses. Giving money to hospitals was an important act of charity, and from the 12th century onward it was a common bequest in last wills.

Muslim Hospitals

Medicine was a major field of study among medieval Muslim scholars. Muslim medical knowledge expanded on the works of ancient Greek authors, such as Hippocrates and Galen, which had largely been lost to the west.

During the Abbasid period (about 750–1258) the Muslims founded many schools of medicine and hospitals, most notably in Baghdad, Córdoba, and Damascus. In 931 Baghdad alone had 860 practicing doctors. The Persian physician al-Razi (died about 925) was the head of the main hospital in Baghdad. Al-Razi wrote some 120 medical books, including pioneering studies of smallpox and measles.

This hospital in Tonnerre, France, was founded in 1293 by Marguerite of Burgundy, the sister-in-law of King Louis IX of France.

LEPER HOSPITALS

Leprosy, an infectious skin disease that leads to paralysis, was widespread in medieval Europe and reached its peak in the 12th and 13th centuries, when leper hospitals were founded in large numbers. In 1227 Louis VIII of France left 100 sous to each of the 2,000 leper hospitals within the kingdom. Lepers were seen as social outcasts and were treated as scapegoats during times of crisis, such as famines. From 1179 leper hospitals (which were always sited outside the town boundaries) were built as closed worlds, complete with churches, chapels, and cemeteries. Lepers were confined to the hospital grounds and, if they chose to venture out, were forced to shake a rattle to alert people to their approach.

SEE ALSO

♦ Charity
♦ Crusader States
♦ Disease
♦ Islamic Scholarship
♦ Medicine
♦ Monasteries

GLOSSARY

A.D. Anno Domini ("the year of our Lord") was the year that Christ was born. All dates with these letters written after them are measured forward from his birth to the present day.

alms Money, food, or gifts given to the poor.

apprentice Someone legally bound for a period of years to a craftsman in order to learn a craft.

aristocracy A privileged section of society, also called the nobility, whose members attained their position through birth rather than merit.

barbarian A name often given to peoples who did not belong to a particular civilization and were considered to be savage and backward.

B.C. Before Christ All dates with these letters written after them are measured backward from Christ's birth date.

blasphemy Words or actions disrespectful to sacred figures, beliefs, or objects.

bureaucracy A part of government relying on specialized administrators and hierarchies (ranks) of officials; characterized by a large amount of paperwork and many regulations.

Buddhism An Indian religion following the teaching of the Buddha (enlightened one), based on the idea that humans can be freed from suffering by self-purification, known as enlightenment.

caliph An Islamic ruler.

caravan A group of people traveling together with animals to carry their goods.

charter A grant of rights and privileges given by a ruler to an individual, community, or nation.

classical A term referring to the cultures of ancient Greece and Rome.

Crusade A military expedition undertaken by European Christians to capture the Holy Land from the Muslims.

diocese The name of a territory under the control of a bishop.

doctrine A specific principle or belief, or a system of beliefs, taught by the church.

dynasty A series of rulers from the same family.

excommunication A decree issued by the Roman Catholic church that prevents an individual from taking part in any sacraments or rites.

heresy A belief contrary to the accepted teachings and beliefs of a religion.

icon A holy image of a sacred figure or event depicted in a stylized way and used during worship in the Orthodox church.

imam An Islamic leader of prayers at a mosque.

infidel Term used by Christians to describe non-Christians.

Islam The Muslim religion based on the teachings of the Prophet Muhammad as laid out in the holy book of the Koran, the basic principle of which is submission to God.

mercenary A soldier who will fight for any employer in return for wages.

Muslim A follower of Islam.

nomads People who wander from place to place rather than living in a settled community.

patriarch The title given to a few powerful church leaders: the bishops of Antioch, Rome, Alexandria, Constantinople, and Jerusalem.

philosophy A search for truth or wisdom through logical reasoning; also the beliefs of an individual or group.

pilgrimage A long journey made to a sacred place as an act of religious devotion.

sacrament A Christian rite, or ceremony, that is an outward sign of inner faith.

Saracen A name used in the Middle Ages for an Arab or a Muslim.

secular Belonging to the civil rather than the church authorities.

siege A military blockade of a fortress or a city in order to force it to surrender, often by cutting off its supplies of food and water.

theology A field of study devoted to religious faith.

tithe A tax of one-tenth of a person's annual produce or income payable to the local church.

tribute A payment made by a subject or nation in recognition of an overlord's power.

usury The name given to charging interest on a loan, a practice that was considered sinful by the medieval church.

vernacular The native or local language of an area, for example, French in France, as opposed to an official language, such as Latin.

TIMELINE

306	Constantine I becomes emperor of Rome
330	Constantine moves his capital from Rome to Byzantium
410	Visigoths sack Rome
c.431	Saint Patrick introduces Christianity to Ireland
434	Attila becomes leader of the Huns
451	Coptic church splits from Orthodox church
452	Attila the Hun invades Italy
476	Romulus Augustulus, last emperor of western Roman Empire, deposed
527	Justinian becomes emperor of eastern Roman Empire
529	Saint Benedict establishes monastery at Monte Cassino
531	Khosrow I begins rule of Sassanid Empire
581	China unified under the Sui dynasty
590	Gregory the Great becomes pope
618	T'ang dynasty established in China
622	Muhammad's flight from Mecca to Medina, later known as the *hegira*
633	Islamic Empire begins to expand across Middle East
638	Muslims under Umar I occupy Jerusalem
661	Mu'awiyah makes Damascus capital of the Umayyad Empire
676	Peninsula of Korea united under kings of Silla
681	First Bulgar state formed
705	Construction of Great Mosque of Damascus begins
711	Muslims begin conquest of Spain
720	Illuminated manuscript of Lindisfarne Gospels produced
726	Venice elects first doge; Byzantine emperor Leo III orders that all icons be destroyed
750	Abbasids overthrow Umayyad dynasty
754	Pope crowns Pippin III as king of the Franks
778	Construction of Borobudur begins
790	Offa's Dyke built to separate England from Wales
793	Norsemen attack Lindisfarne, England, in one of the first Viking raids
794	Emperor Kammu of Japan moves capital to Heian
800	Charlemagne crowned emperor of the Romans by pope in Rome
c. 802	Jayavarman II unifies Khmer peoples
863	Missionaries Cyril and Methodius begin to convert Slavs to Christianity
871	Alfred the Great becomes king of Wessex
882	Oleg makes Kiev capital of Rus
885	Vikings begin siege of Paris
c. 896	Magyars settle in Hungary
910	Cluny monastery founded in Burgundy
911	Charles III grants area of land—later called Normandy—to Viking leader Rollo
918	Wang Kon founds kingdom of Koryo
939	State of Annam becomes independent from China
c. 950	Harold Bluetooth unites Denmark
955	German knights defeat Magyars at Battle of Lechfeld
960	Sung dynasty gain power in China
982	Erik the Red sets out on first expedition to Greenland
987	Hugh Capet becomes king of France, founding Capetian dynasty
988	Vladimir I of Kiev converts to Christianity
c. 1000	Leif Eriksson lands on coast of Newfoundland
1000	Stephen I becomes first king of Hungary
1014	Byzantine emperor Basil II defeats Bulgarians at Serres
1016	King Canute of Denmark seizes throne of England
c. 1040	Movable-type printing develops in China
1054	Orthodox, or Eastern, church splits from Roman Catholic church
1055	Seljuk Turks take control of Baghdad
1066	William the Conqueror defeats Anglo-Saxons at Battle of Hastings
1071	Seljuk Turks defeat Byzantines at Battle of Manzikert
1096	Start of First Crusade
1099	City of Jerusalem falls to Crusaders
c. 1119	Knights Templar established
1130	Roger II crowned king of Sicily
1147	Start of Second Crusade
c. 1150	Gothic style of architecture begins to appear in Europe
1154	Henry II becomes first Plantagenet king of England;

TIMELINE

	Arab scholar al-Idrisi creates map of known world	1248	Start of Seventh Crusade		Chinese Ming dynasty established
1155	Frederick I becomes Holy Roman emperor, the first ruler to hold the title	1250	Mamluk general Aibak seizes power in Egypt	1377	Pope Gregory XI calls for arrest of John Wycliffe for heresy
1158	First university founded at Bologna	1252	Pope Innocent IV authorizes use of torture against suspected heretics	1378	Beginning of Great Schism
1170	Archbishop of Canterbury Thomas Becket is murdered	1258	Mongols capture Baghdad	1380	Dmitry Donskoy defeats Mongols at Battle of Kulikovo
1171	Saladin becomes sultan of Egypt	1260	Cairo becomes capital of Mamluk Empire; Mamluks defeat Mongols at Battle of Ain Jalut	1381	Peasants' Revolt breaks out in England
1187	Saladin recaptures Jerusalem for Muslims, triggering Third Crusade in 1189	1271	Marco Polo embarks on journey to court of Kublai Khan	c. 1385	Geoffrey Chaucer begins work on *Canterbury Tales*
1192	Minamoto Yoritomo becomes shogun of Japan	1274	Pope Gregory X recognizes Rudolf I as first Hapsburg Holy Roman emperor	1386	Duke Jagiello of Lithuania becomes king of Poland, starting new dynasty
1204	Crusaders capture Constantinople	c. 1275	Formation of Hanseatic League	1396	Ottoman sultan Bayezid I defeats crusaders at Battle of Nicopolis
1206	Mongol chieftain Temüjin takes the title Genghis Khan, or Universal Ruler; Qutbud-Din founds sultanate of Delhi	1279	Kublai Khan establishes Yüan dynasty in China	1397	Sweden, Norway, and Denmark are united under Union of Kalmar
		1291	Crusaders finally leave Palestine		
1209	Start of Albigensian Crusade; Followers of Saint Francis form the Friars Minor	1297	William Wallace leads Scottish rebellion against King Edward I of England	1401	Tamerlane sacks Damascus
				1410	Teutonic Knights defeated at Battle of Tannenberg
1215	Magna Carta granted by King John I of England; Pope Innocent III frees Christians from financial debts to Jews; Mongol forces destroy Chinese city of Chengdu	1302	Flemish footsoldiers defeat French knights at Battle of Courtrai; First Estates General held in France	1415	Jan Hus executed for heresy; English forces under Henry V defeat French at Agincourt
				1429	Joan of Arc leads French army to victory at Orléans
		1307	Dante begins work on *The Divine Comedy*	1453	Constantinople falls to Ottoman Turks under Mehmed II
1216	Dominican order founded	1309	Popes move to Avignon	1455	Start of Wars of the Roses; Invention of Gutenberg system of printing
1226	Louis IX becomes king of France	1312	Mansa Musa becomes king of Mali		
1230	Guillaume de Lorris begins to write the *Romance of the Rose*	1314	Robert Bruce defeats Edward II at Bannockburn	1462	Ivan the Great becomes grand prince of Moscow
		1336	Hindu kingdom of Vijayanagara founded in India	1485	Henry VII becomes first Tudor king of England
1231	Pope Gregory IX authorizes inquisition against heretics			1492	Christian forces conquer Granada
1233	Teutonic Knights begin conquest of Prussia	1337	Start of Hundred Years' War between England and France	1493	Muhammad Askia begins rule of Songhai Empire
1238	Nasrid dynasty take over kingdom of Granada	1346	First recorded use of gunpowder weapons in Europe at Battle of Crécy		
1240	Mongols destroy Kiev			1504	Michelangelo completes his marble statue of David
1242	Alexander Nevsky defeats Teutonic Knights	1347	Black Death arrives in Europe	1517	Ottoman sultan Selim I defeats Mamluks to take control of Syria and Egypt
1243	Mongols defeat Seljuk Turks at Battle of Kosedagh	1368	Mongols lose control of northern China;		

Further Reading

Books

Aldred, D.H., *Castles and Cathedrals: The Architecture of Power 1066–1550*. New York: Cambridge University Press, 1993.

Allan, T., *Legends of Chivalry: Medieval Myth*. Alexandria, VA: Time Life Inc., 2000.

Bingham, J., Gower J., and Wood G., *Medieval World*. London, UK: Usborne Publishing Ltd, 1999.

Breuilly, E., O'Brien, J., and Palmer, M., *Religions of the World: The Illustrated Guide to Origins, Beliefs, Traditions, and Festivals*. New York: Checkmark Books, 1997.

Bull, S., *An Historical Guide to Arms and Armor*. New York: Facts on File, 1991.

Corbishley, M., *The Middle Ages: A Cultural Atlas for Young People*. New York: Facts on File, 1990.

Corrain, L., Ricciardi, S., and Ricciardi A., *Giotto and Medieval Art: The Lives and Works of Medieval Artists*. New York: Peter Bedrick Books, 1995.

Gies, F. and J., *Cathedral, Forge, and Waterwheel: Technology and Invention in the Middle Ages*. New York: HarperPerennial Library, 1995.

Gimpel, J., *The Medieval Machine: The Industrial Revolution of the Middle Ages*. New York: Penguin USA, 1977.

Grant, N., *The Vikings*. New York: Oxford University Press, 1998.

Gravett, C., and Dann, F., *Eyewitness: Castle*. New York: DK Publishing, 2000.

Gravett, C., and Dann, F., *Eyewitness: Knight*. New York: DK Publishing, 2000.

Gregory, T., *The Dark Ages*. New York: Facts on File, 1993.

Hanawalt, B.A., *The Middle Ages: An Illustrated History*. New York: Oxford University Press, 1998.

Haywood, J., *The Medieval World (World Atlas of the Past, Volume 2)*. New York: Oxford University Press, 2000.

Hicks, P., *How Castles Were Built*. Austin, TX: Raintree/Steck Vaughn, 1998.

Hicks, P., *Technology in the Time of the Vikings*. Austin, TX: Raintree/Steck Vaughn, 1998.

Hinds, K., *The City (Life in the Middle Ages)*. Tarrytown, NY: Benchmark Books, 2000.

Hinds, K., *The Countryside (Life in the Middle Ages)*. Tarrytown, NY: Benchmark Books, 2000.

Jones, P.M., *Medieval Medicine in Illuminated Manuscripts*. London, UK: British Library Publications, 1999.

Jordan, W.C., *The Middle Ages: A Watts Guide for Children*. Danbury, CT: Franklin Watts Inc., 2000.

Langley, A., *Eyewitness: Medieval Life*. New York: DK Publishing, 2000.

Langley, A., and Dennis, P., *DK Discoveries: Castles at War*. New York: DK Publishing, 2000.

MacDonald, F., *Marco Polo: A Journey through China*. Danbury, CT: Franklin Watts Inc., 1998.

MacDonald, F., *The Middle Ages*. New York: Facts on File, 1993.

MacDonald, F., *The World in the Time of Charlemagne*. Broomall, PA: Chelsea House Publishing, 2000.

MacDonald, F., and Bergin, M., *A Medieval Castle*. New York: Peter Bedrick Books, 1993.

MacDonald, F., and James, J., *A Medieval Cathedral*. New York: Peter Bedrick Books, 1991.

Margeson, S.M., and Anderson, P., *Eyewitness: Viking*. New York: DK Publishing, 2000.

Marshall, C., *Warfare in the Medieval World*. Austin, TX: Raintree/Steck Vaughn, 1998.

Martell, H., *The World of Islam before 1700*. Austin, TX: Raintree/Steck Vaughn, 1998.

McNeill, S., *The Middle Ages*. New York: Oxford University Press, 1998.

Power, E.E., *Medieval Women*. New York: Cambridge University Press, 1997.

Roden, K., *The Plague*. Providence, RI: Copper Beech Books, 1996.

Sheehan, S., *Great African Kingdoms*. Austin, TX: Raintree/Steck Vaughn, 1999.

Shuter, J., *The Middle Ages*. Westport, CT: Heinemann Library, 1999.

Simpson, J., and Michaelson, C., *Ancient China*. Alexandria, VA: Time Life Inc, 1996.

Stetoff, R., and Goetzmann, W.H., *Marco Polo and the Medieval Explorers*. Broomall, PA: Chelsea House Publishing, 1992.

Williams, B., *Ancient China*. New York: Viking Children's Books, 1996.

Websites

1000 AD
www.channel4.co.uk/nextstep/1000ad

BBC Online: History
www.bbc.co.uk/history

The Black Death
www.discovery.com/stories/history/blackdeath/blackdeath.html

Byzantium 1200
www.byzantium1200.org

The Entire Bayeux Tapestry
members.tripod.com/~mr_sedivy/med_bay.html

History of Britain
www.bbc.co.uk/history/programmes/hob

History of India
www.historyofindia.com

Islam: Empire of Faith
www.pbs.org/empires/islam

The Land of Genghis Khan
www.nationalgeographic.com/features/97/genghis

Secrets of Lost Empires: A Medieval Siege
www.pbs.org/wgbh/nova/lostempires/trebuchet

The Vikings
www.pbs.org/wgbh/nova/vikings

Set Index

Numbers in **bold type** are volume numbers.

Page numbers in *italics* refer to pictures or their captions.

A
Abbasid dynasty **3**:29, 46, **5**:45, 46–47, 48
   literature **6**:30
   medical schools **4**:68
   and Persia **8**:23–24
   See also Baghdad
abbeys **7**:19
Abd ar-Rahman, *Arab ruler* **4**:38
Abelard **1**:*4*, 55 **8**:58, **9**:17
Abul Kasim **6**:64
accounting **7**:27
Acre **3**:15, 17, 21, **10**:44
Adrian I, *pope* **5**:50, **8**:8
Adrian IV, *pope* **4**:19
adultery **3**:*7*, *9*, **10**:62
Africa **1**:5–11
   gold from **7**:12
   and the Islamic Empire **1**:6, 7–8, 10–11, **2**:60, **6**:8, 68
   Kilwa **1**:5, **6**:8–9
   North **1**:5–6, **6**:68
   salt from **7**:12
   slavery **9**:33
Agincourt, Battle of **5**:11–12, **10**:53
agriculture **1**:*12*–15, **3**:24
   crop failures **2**:62
   fields **8**:*47*, 48
   and horses **1**:12, **4**:65, 66, **10**:5–6
   labor riots **10**:7
   in monasteries **7**:22, **10**:6–7
   plows **1**:*12*, **4**:65, 66, **8**:*18*, 19, **10**:*4*, 5–6
   and the seasons **2**:62
   and women **10**:*41*, 59
   See also livestock; plows
Aibak, *ruler of Egypt* **6**:47
Aidan, St. **7**:16
Aix-la-Chapelle (Aachen) **2**:37, **10**:67
Ajanta Caves **5**:25
Alani **1**:51–52, **5**:15
Albert I, *Holy Roman emperor* **4**:51–52
Albert V, *duke of Austria* **4**:52
Albertus Magnus, St. **9**:*18*
Albigensian Crusade **3**:16, **4**:14, 58, **5**:31, **6**:50
Albigensians (Cathars) **4**:22, 58, **5**:*31*, **6**:50
Alcázar **9**:42
alchemy **6**:43, 65, **9**:*21*
Alcuin **2**:37, **10**:67
Alexander III, *pope* **4**:19
Alexander V, *pope* **4**:41
Alexander VI, *pope* **4**:59, **8**:7
Alexander Nevsky **9**:8
Alexius I Comnenus, *Byzantine emperor* **3**:17, 18, 19
Alfonso VI, *king of León and Castile* **9**:46
Alfonso VIII, *king of Castile* **9**:45
Alfonso Henriques **9**:46
Alfred the Great, *king of Wessex* **1**:*16*, **3**:39–40, 51, **6**:33
algebra **5**:48
Alhambra palace **5**:*7*, 43
Alhazen **9**:20
Ali ar-Rida, tomb **8**:24
Almagest **1**:34

Almohads **1**:6, **4**:38, **6**:46, **9**:43, 45
Almoravids **1**:6, **9**:43
Alp-Arslan, *Seljuk sultan* **10**:25–26
alphabets **10**:65–66
   runic **9**:*13*, **10**:39
althing **8**:*17*, **9**:15, **10**:38
Ambrose of Milan, St. **7**:19
Amiens Cathedral **2**:26
Amr ibn al-As **2**:10
Anacletus II, *pope* **8**:61
Andalusia **4**:38, **9**:42–43
Andrew II, *king of Hungary* **5**:14
Andrew Bogolyubsky **6**:7, **9**:7
Angevins **1**:*17*, **4**:*13*, **7**:48
Angkor Wat **9**:39, *40*
Angles **1**:52, **9**:24
Anglo-Saxon (language) **6**:19
Anglo-Saxon Chronicle **6**:25
Anglo-Saxons **1**:*18*–19, 52 **3**:51
   literature **6**:26
   See also Alfred the Great
Annam **9**:40–41
Anselm of Canterbury **8**:58, 66, **9**:17
Anselm of Laon **9**:*17*
Ansgar, St. **9**:15
Anthony of Egypt, St. **7**:18–*19*
Anthony, St. (Anthony of Thebes) **3**:*4*
Antioch **3**:12, 15, 19, **7**:48, **10**:28
anti-Semitism *See* Jews and Judaism
Antwerp **1**:62, **6**:40
Aquinas, Thomas *See* Thomas Aquinas
Aquitaine **4**:14, **5**:10, 11
Arabic **5**:41, 48, **6**:19–20, 29, **10**:66
   writing **6**:*20*, **10**:66, 68
Arabs **1**:20–21
   explorers **3**:56–57
   mapmakers **3**:57, **6**:56
   medicine **6**:65
   pottery **8**:41
   sailors **3**:56–58
   science and mathematics **9**:19–20
   ships and seafaring **9**:27, 28
   technology **10**:4
   trade and merchants **1**:21, **7**:6
   women **10**:64
   See also Islamic Empire
Aragon **6**:68, **9**:47
archery **9**:48, 49
architecture **1**:22–27
   Byzantine **2**:8
   Gothic cathedrals **2**:*23*, *25*, 26–28, **7**:67–68, **8**:14
   Islamic **5**:*7*, 42–43, *46*
   Mamluk **6**:48
   mosque **5**:*41*, *46*, **6**:48
   Romanesque **2**:24–26, **7**:48
   in the Spanish kingdoms **9**:46
   See also building techniques; castles and fortifications; cathedrals; houses and homes
Ardahang (book) **6**:50
Arians and Arianism **4**:57, **9**:42
Aristotle **1**:38, 39, **8**:54–55, **9**:17–18, 23, 68
Arius **4**:57
Arles, Kingdom of **1**:67
Armenia **1**:28–29, **6**:50
Armenian church **1**:29
arms, coats of **4**:55, *56*, **7**:42
arms and armor **1**:*30*–33, **4**:55, **10**:50
   bows **1**:32–33, **4**:66, **5**:11–12, **10**:50

   iron used in **6**:53, 54
   lances **2**:*51*
   Mongol **7**:30–31
   suits of armor **1**:32, **6**:*10*, **7**:8
   See also gunpowder; guns; metalwork; warfare
Arnulf, *duke of Carinthia* **6**:45
Arpád **5**:13, **6**:45
Árpád dynasty **5**:13–14
Arthur, *British king* **4**:*36*, **6**:13
arts and crafts
   guilds and **4**:48
   Islamic **5**:42–43
   Japanese **5**:56, *59*
   Korean **6**:*17*
   Viking **10**:39
   See also jewelry; painting and sculpture
Ash'ari, al- **8**:55
Ashikaga clan **5**:59
Ashikaga Yoshimitsu, *shogun of Japan* **5**:54
Ashkenazim **5**:67
Ashot I, *king of Armenia* **1**:29
Ashot II, *king of Armenia* **1**:29
Ashot III, *king of Armenia* **1**:28, 29
assemblies, national **4**:36–37
astrolabes **1**:*36*, **9**:28
astrology **6**:43, 63, **9**:22
astronomy **1**:34–37, **9**:19–20
Asturias **9**:43–45
Athelstan, *king of England* **1**:19
Athos, Mount **4**:43, **7**:50
Attila, *king of the Huns* **2**:29, **5**:16
Augustine of Hippo, St. **7**:19, 20, **8**:35, 57, *63*, **9**:17, 32
Augustine, St. **5**:18, **7**:16
Augustinians **4**:21, 23
Augustus, Romulus *See* Romulus Augustulus
auto-da-fé **4**:58, **5**:*30*
Autun **1**:*67*–68, **7**:*66*
Avars **4**:29
Averroës (Ibn Rushd) **1**:38, **8**:55, 56
Avicenna (Ibn Sina) **1**:*39*, **5**:48, **6**:65, **8**:24, 55, **9**:18
Avignon **4**:40, *41*, **8**:7
Axum **1**:*10*

B
Babel, Tower of **1**:23, **6**:*18*
Babur **5**:29
Bacon, Roger **9**:23
Baghdad **1**:40–41, **3**:44, 46, **9**:55, **10**:25
Bagratid family **1**:29
Bahmani Sultanate **5**:28
Balathista, Battle of **2**:9
Baldwin I, *emperor of Constantinople* (Baldwin IX, *count of Flanders*) **6**:40
Baldwin I, *king of Jerusalem* **3**:12, *13*
Baliol, John de, *king of Scotland* **3**:68
Balkans **1**:42–45, **7**:55
   See also Slavic peoples
ball games **3**:26, **9**:49–50
Baltic States **1**:46–49
Balts **1**:46, **4**:31–32
banks **7**:5, 6, 26, 27, 28
Bannockburn, Battle of **9**:25
Bantu **1**:5, *9*
barbarian invasions **1**:50–53, **8**:34, *9*:4
Barcelona **2**:28, **6**:68

Bari, Battle of **2**:8–9
Barovier family **4**:*34*
Basel, Council of **4**:60
Basil I, *Byzantine emperor* **2**:8
Basil II, *Byzantine emperor* **2**:8, *9*
Basil of Caesarea, St. **4**:67, **7**:50
Batu **9**:7–8
Baybars I, *Mamluk sultan* **2**:11, **3**:21
Bayeux Tapestry **3**:*50*, **7**:*45*
Bayezid I, "the Thunderbolt," *Ottoman sultan* **7**:55, 58
bear-baiting **9**:51
Beaumaris Castle **1**:*23*, 64, **2**:20, **10**:*47*
Beauvais Cathedral **1**:*24*, 27, **2**:26
Becket, St. Thomas **3**:*53*–54, **8**:28, *66*
Bede, the Venerable **1**:19, **4**:62, **7**:*13*, **9**:22
Bedouin **5**:44
beggars **7**:59
Beijing **2**:50
   Forbidden City **2**:*48*, 50
Béla III, *king of Hungary* **5**:14
Béla IV, *king of Hungary* **5**:14
Belgium *See* Low Countries
Belisarius **6**:4
Benedict XIII, *antipope* **4**:41
Benedictines
   hospitals **4**:68
   monasteries **2**:63–64, **7**:21, 48
Benedict of Nursia, St. **1**:*54*, 56, **3**:38, **7**:13, 20, *21*
Benin **1**:5, *9*
Beowulf (poem) **6**:26
Berbers **1**:5, **4**:38, **5**:46
Berengar, *king of Italy* **6**:45
Bernard of Clairvaux, St. **1**:*4*, 55, **7**:15, *21*, **8**:*66*
Bible, translations **4**:59, *60*, **6**:19, **10**:68
Biel, Gabriel **8**:58
Bilikt Khan **7**:32
bills of exchange **7**:5–6, 27–28, **10**:20
Bishoi, St. **3**:*4*
bishops **2**:54, **8**:35, 43, 44, 64–65
   Orthodox **8**:46
Black Death (plague) **1**:56–58, **2**:59, 62, **3**:31, 32, 62, **6**:31, 43, 65 **8**:*37*, 39
blacksmiths **6**:53, 54, **10**:42, *63*
Blanche of Castile **6**:35
blast furnaces **6**:53
Bleda, *king of the Huns* **5**:15–16
blood feuds **10**:46
Blood Libel **5**:64
Boccaccio **1**:58, **6**:29
Boethius **8**:57, **9**:17
Bogomils **6**:50
Bohemia **1**:59–60
   See also Hus, Jan; Prague
Bohemond **3**:15
Boleslaw I, "the Brave," *king of Poland* **8**:31
Boleslaw III, *king of Poland* **8**:32
Boniface VIII, *pope* **4**:15, **6**:23, **8**:26, 65
Boniface IX, *pope* **4**:41
Boniface, St. **6**:39, **7**:16, *17*
bookkeeping **7**:5, 27
Book of Giants **6**:50
Book of Healing, The **1**:39
Book of Kells **5**:22, 33
Book of Kings **6**:29
Book of the Order of Chivalry **2**:52

73

Book of Roger, The **6**:56
Book of Secrets **6**:50
Book of Sentences, The **8**:58
Book of Three Virtues **2**:53
books **5**:23, **10**:31
  See also Koran; paper and printing
Books of Hours **2**:12, **3**:25, **5**:23, **6**:63, **8**:18, 27
Borgia family **8**:7
Bosworth Field, Battle of **3**:54, **10**:56
bowls **9**:50
bows **1**:32–33, **4**:66, **5**:11–12, **9**:48
Brahmins **8**:46
Brendan (Irish monk) **3**:58
Breton Lais **6**:27
Brian Boru, *king of Ireland* **5**:34
Britons **1**:18, 52, **9**:24
Bruges **1**:24, 61–62, **2**:66, **6**:38, 40, 52, **10**:14
Brunelleschi, Filippo **4**:4, **8**:60
Brussels, town hall **1**:24
Budapest **5**:13, 14
Buddha (Siddartha Gautama) **5**:25, **7**:22, **8**:29–30, 51, 59, **9**:41
Buddhism **2**:34, 45, **5**:24, 55, 56, **7**:14, 22, **8**:29–30, 43, 51, 52, **9**:39, 41
building techniques **1**:27, 63–66
  scaffolding **1**:26, 66
  See also architecture; castles and fortifications; cathedrals
Bukhari, Isma'il al- **5**:40
Bulgars **1**:43, 44, **2**:9, **9**:35
Burgos Cathedral **2**:28
Burgundy **1**:67–68, **5**:68, **6**:41, **8**:16
Burmans **9**:40
Bursa **7**:54
bushido **5**:56
Buyids **5**:47, **10**:25
Byzantine Empire (Eastern Roman Empire) **2**:4–9, **5**:44, **8**:67
  clothing **3**:37
  coins **7**:24
  education **3**:42–43
  the emperor **8**:33–34
  and Greece **4**:43
  and the Huns **5**:16
  in Italy **5**:49
  landowners **8**:47
  language **6**:18, 19
  legal system **6**:22
  literature **6**:29
  marriage **6**:59–60
  mosaics **7**:33, 34
  public baths **5**:5
  and religion **2**:7–8
  and the Seljuk Turks **1**:44, **2**:9, 30, **3**:17, **10**:26
  towns and cities **10**:13
  trade **2**:6–7, **10**:19
  and the Venetians **10**:35
  See also Orthodox church
Byzantium See Constantinople

C
Cairo **2**:10–11, **3**:44, 46, **7**:35
Calais **5**:10–11, 12
calendars and clocks **2**:12–13
calligraphy **5**:23, **10**:68
Cambodia **9**:39
canals **10**:23–24
cannons **2**:21, **10**:8, 50, 52, 53
canonization **7**:13
Canon Law **6**:22–23
Canon of Medicine (book) **1**:39, **5**:48, **6**:65
Canterbury **2**:26, **8**:66
  pilgrimages to **2**:65, **3**:53, **8**:28–29, **10**:22
Canterbury Tales, The (book) **2**:38, 65, **8**:28–29
Canute, *king of England* **3**:51
Capellanus, Andreas **3**:7

Capetians **2**:14, **4**:12–13, **8**:13
  See also Louis IX
caravels **9**:29
cards, playing **9**:52
Carmelites **4**:21, 22–23
Carolingian minuscule **2**:37, **10**:67, 68
Carolingian Renaissance **2**:37
Carolingians **4**:18, **7**:46, **10**:34
  coinage **7**:24
carpets and rugs **2**:15–16
carracks **9**:29
Carthusians **4**:24, **7**:21
Casimir I, *king of Poland* **8**:32
Casimir III, *king of Poland* **8**:32
Casimir IV, *king of Poland* **1**:48
Castile **4**:39, **9**:42, 45, 47
Castillon, Battle of **5**:12
castles and fortifications **1**:22–23, **2**:17–22
Catalaunian Plains, Battle of the **5**:16
cataphracts **10**:49
Cathars See Albigensians
cathedrals **1**:24, **2**:23–28, **4**:4
  Orthodox **7**:53
  schools **3**:40
Catherine, St. **7**:14
Catholicism See Roman Catholic church
cattle **1**:15, **6**:31
Causa et curae (book) **4**:61
cavalry **6**:10–12, 14, **10**:49, 50
celadon **6**:17, **8**:41
Celts **1**:52, **7**:62
Central Asian peoples **2**:29–30
  See also Huns; Magyars; Mongols; Turkic peoples
Chandragupta II, *Gupta king* **5**:24, 25
Ch'ang-an **2**:31–32, 45, 47, **10**:13
chansons de geste **6**:59
charity **2**:33–34, **7**:59
  See also hospitals
Charlemagne, *king of the Franks and Holy Roman emperor* **2**:7, 35–37, **3**:35, 39 **4**:18, 29–30, 63, **5**:50–51, **6**:43 **8**:8, 34, 60
Charles I, *king of Bohemia* **9**:37
Charles III, "the Simple," *Carolingian king* **7**:46
Charles IV, *Holy Roman emperor* **1**:60
Charles IV, "the Bald," *king of France* **2**:14, **4**:13, **5**:10, **6**:39–40
Charles V, *Holy Roman emperor* **4**:64
Charles V, *king of France* **5**:11, **8**:34
Charles VI, *king of France* **3**:31, **5**:11
Charles VII, *king of France* **5**:11, 12, 68
Charles of Anjou **1**:17, **4**:28
Charles the Bold, *duke of Burgundy* **1**:67, 68, **8**:16
Charles of Navarre **8**:21
Charles Robert, *king of Hungary* **5**:14
charms, lucky **6**:43
Chartres Cathedral **1**:25, **2**:23, 24, 26, 27, **4**:47
Château de Saumur **2**:22
Château Gaillard **2**:19
Chaucer, Geoffrey **2**:38, 65, **6**:25–26, **8**:29
Cheng Ho **2**:50, **3**:58, **6**:9, **9**:28
chess **9**:49, 52
childbirth **10**:60, 61
children **2**:39–42, **10**:62
  becoming knights **2**:40, 52, **6**:12
  peasant **2**:42, **8**:19
  slaves **9**:30–31
  See also apprentices; education; toys and games

China **2**:43–50
  astronomy **1**:35
  canals **10**:24
  Ch'ang-an **2**:31–32, 45, 47, **10**:13
  Christian missionaries **7**:17
  daily life **2**:45, **3**:26
  dynasties **8**:36
  education **10**:33
  emperors **8**:36
  examination system **3**:42
  exploration from **3**:58
  Five Dynasties and Ten Kingdoms **2**:48
  furnishings **5**:6
  Grand Canal **2**:44, 47
  Great Wall **2**:43, 47
  houses **5**:7
  influence on Japan **5**:55
  inventions **9**:22, **10**:4
  language **6**:20
  literature **6**:30
  mapmaking **6**:55
  metal reserves **7**:12
  Ming dynasty **2**:47, 49, 50, **8**:19
  money **7**:28
  and the Mongols See Mongols
  paper and printing **2**:48, **8**:11–12
  peasants **8**:19
  postal system **2**:66
  pottery **2**:31, 45, 50, **8**:40–41
  rice **1**:14, **2**:43, 48
  science **9**:22
  ships and boats **2**:49, **9**:27–28
  silk **9**:62–63
  slavery **9**:33
  Sui dynasty **2**:43–45
  Sung dynasty **2**:47, 48–49, **3**:26, **4**:37, **7**:28, **8**:19, 36, 40, **10**:64
  T'ang dynasty **2**:31, 45–48, 66, **3**:42, **6**:30
  taxation **9**:57
  towns and cities **10**:13
  trade **2**:45–47, **10**:19
  warfare **9**:22
  washing and sanitation **5**:5
  women **2**:49, **10**:04
  writing **6**:20, **10**:65, 68
  Yüan dynasty **2**:49–50, **8**:19, 40
Ch'in Shih Huang Ti, *emperor of China* **8**:36
Chioggia, Battle of **5**:52, **6**:67
chivalry **2**:51–52, **6**:36
Chrétien de Troyes **6**:27
Christian Instruction (book) **8**:63
Christianity See church, Christian
Christine de Pisan **2**:53
Chrysostom, St. John **7**:50
church, Christian **2**:54–56
  attitude to magic **6**:42, 43
  Canon Law **6**:22–23
  and charity **2**:33
  church time **2**:12
  and drama **9**:65, 66
  Easter **7**:63
  embroidery for **3**:49–50
  feasts **3**:25–26, 63
  and heaven and hell **4**:53–54
  illuminated manuscripts **5**:22–23
  and Jerusalem **5**:60–61
  Jews in Christian lands **5**:63–64, 65
  and kings **8**:35
  language and **6**:19
  metal religious objects **7**:9
  miracles and mysticism **7**:13–15
  missionaries **7**:16–17
  music **7**:38–39
  and the Normans **7**:48
  paintings and sculptures **7**:65, 66, 67–68
  philosophy **8**:57–58
  priests and clergy **8**:43, 44–46
  replacing paganism **7**:63
  tithes **9**:57, **10**:41

and the universe **1**:34–35
and village life **10**:40–41
in Wales **10**:48
and witchcraft **3**:10
and women **10**:59
year **2**:12
  See also charity; friars; heresy; inquisition; monasteries; Nestorian church, Orthodox church ; priests and clergy; Roman Catholic church
Chu Yüan-chang **2**:49, **8**:19
ciompi, revolt **4**:46, **8**:20
Cistercians **1**:13, 68, **3**:38, **7**:21, 22
  monastery at Clairvaux **10**:6–7
cities See towns and cities
City of God, The (book) **8**:35, 63, **9**:32
city-states **2**:57–60, **4**:37, **10**:14–15
Clairvaux, monastery **10**:6–7
Clare, St. **10**:60
Clement III, *pope* **8**:6
Clement V, *pope* **4**:15, 40, **8**:7
Clement VII, *antipope*, and the Great Schism, **4**:40–41
Clermont, Council of **3**:17–18
climate and seasons **2**:61–62
clocks **2**:13
Clontarf, Battle of **5**:34
clothing See dress
Clotilda **4**:18
Clovis, *king of the Franks* **1**:53, **4**:17–18, **8**:13
Cluniacs **1**:68, **8**:30
Cluny **1**:68, **2**:63–64, **7**:21
Cnut, *king of England* **1**:19
coal, mining **7**:12
cock-fighting **9**:51
codex **8**:12
cogs (ships) **9**:28–29
coins **7**:23–24, 25–26, 28
Cola (Chola) kingdom **5**:26
Cologne, cathedral **1**:24, **2**:28
Coloman, *king of Hungary* **5**:14
coloni **9**:31
colophons **10**:66
Columba, St. **7**:16, **9**:24
Columbanus, St. **7**:16
Columbus, Christopher **9**:29, **10**:21
Commentary on the Mishna **6**:46
Common Law **3**:53, **6**:23, **8**:48
Common Pleas, Court of **6**:23
communications **2**:65–66
  See also transportation
compasses **3**:58, **9**:28
Confessions (book) **8**:63
Confucianism **2**:48, **6**:17
Conrad III, *king of Germany* **3**:19–20
Conrad IV, *king of Germany* **4**:51
Conrad of Marburg **5**:32
Conrad of Mazovia **8**:32, **9**:60
Constance, Council of **4**:41, 60
Constantine I, "the Great," *Roman emperor* **2**:4–5, 54, 67, **8**:9, 62, 67, 68
Constantine V, *Byzantine emperor* **1**:43
Constantine VI, *Byzantine emperor* **2**:7
Constantine XI, *Byzantine emperor* **2**:9
Constantine, Donation of **8**:9
Constantinople (Byzantium; Istanbul) **2**:4–5, 8, 9, 21, 67–68, **3**:20, 21, **5**:6–7, 47, **6**:5, 67, **7**:4, 9, 55–57, **9**:63, **10**:13, 29,53
convents **10**:60
Copernicus, Nicolaus **1**:37
copper **7**:12
Copts **3**:4–5
Corsica **6**:68
Cortes, the **8**:17
courtly love **3**:6–7, **6**:26, 37, **10**:59

Courtrai, Battle of **1**:*62*, **6**:40–41, **8**:26
Covilhao, Pedro de **1**:9
craftsmen **4**:48, **10**:42–43
Crécy, Battle of **4**:*62*, **5**:10, 11–12, **10**:*50*, *51*
Crete **6**:68
crime and punishment **3**:*8–10*, **6**:22, **10**:*10*, 44
    adultery **3**:*7*, *9*, **10**:*62*
    women debtors **10**:*63*
    See also inquisition; law and legal codes; torture
crops *See* agriculture
crossbows **1**:*33*, **9**:48
Crusaders **3**:*12*, 13–14, *18*, **6**:12
    attack Constantinople (1204) **2**:68, **3**:20, *21*, **6**:67
    castles built by **2**:21
    and Jews **5**:65
    Louis IX **6**:35
    See also Crusades
Crusader states (Latin states) **3**:*12–15*, 19
Crusades **2**:9, **3**:*16–21*, **5**:61, 65, **7**:17
    Albigensian **3**:16, **4**:14, 58, **5**:31, **6**:*50*
    Children's **3**:20
    Fifth **3**:21
    First **3**:12, *19*, 58, **4**:27–28, **8**:5, **10**:*28*
    Fourth **3**:20, **10**:35
    hospitals **4**:68
    Peasants' **3**:18
    Second **3**:14, 19–20
    Seventh **3**:21
    Sixth **3**:21
    Third **3**:15, *19*, 20, **4**:19, **9**:29
    See also Crusaders
curfew **3**:26, **10**:45
Cyril and Methodius, Sts. **1**:43, 59, **7**:17, *52*, 53, **9**:35, 36
Cyzicus, Battle of **2**:6

D

daily life **3**:*22–27*
    in China **2**:45, **3**:*26*
    and the church **2**:56
    of nobility **3**:*22–24*, **7**:*42*
    and the Roman Catholic church **8**:65–66
    in villages **3**:25–26, **8**:48, **10**:*40–43*
    women **3**:25, **10**:*43*, 58–60
    See also children; food and drink; towns and cities
daimyo **5**:57
Damascus **3**:*28–29*, 44, **5**:*42*, 46, **7**:*34*
damask **3**:29, 36
Damietta **3**:21
Dampierre, Guy de **2**:14
dancing **3**:*25*, **7**:*41*, **9**:*67*
Danes **1**:47
danse macabre **1**:*57*, **3**:31
Dante Alighieri **3**:*30*, **4**:4, 54, **6**:*28–29*, 37
David I, *king of Scotland* **9**:24
David, St. **10**:48
Death of Arthur **6**:25, 28
death and burial **3**:31–32
Decameron (book) **1**:58, **6**:29
Decretum **6**:23
deforestation **4**:11, **6**:52
Deir Anba Bishoi **3**:4
Delhi Sultanate **5**:*26*, 27–28
De Materia Medica (book) **6**:65
Denmark **9**:13–15
dental problems **3**:34, **6**:64
dervishes **5**:*39*, **7**:40
Despenser, Hugh Le **10**:*10*
destriers **4**:66
De Variolis et Morbillis **6**:65
Diamond Sutra **8**:11

Diaspora **5**:62
Díaz, Rodrigo (El Cid) **9**:45
dice **9**:52
Diocletian, *Roman emperor* **8**:68
Dioscorides **6**:65
dirhams **7**:23–24
disease **3**:*33–34*, 62, **4**:8, 67, **10**:17
    See also Black Death; hospitals; leprosy and lepers
Divine Comedy, The (poem) **3**:30, **4**:54
divorce **6**:59–60
Dmitry II, *grand prince of Moscow* **9**:9
doges **4**:*37*, **10**:34
Dome of the Rock **5**:*60*, 61, **7**:34
Domesday Book **3**:53, **8**:*38*, 48, 49, **10**:57
Dominicans **4**:21, 22, *23*, **5**:31
Dominic, St. **4**:22, **5**:*31*
Donatello **4**:48
Dover Castle **3**:*51*
dowries **6**:58, 59, **10**:*60*, 64
drafts (checkers) **9**:52
Dream Pool Essays (book) **9**:22
dream-visions **6**:28
dress **3**:35–38, **7**:*43*, 44
dromons **2**:6
Druze religion **3**:47
Duncan I, *king of Scotland* **9**:24
Duns Scotus, John **9**:18
Dunstan, St. **10**:65
Durham Cathedral **2**:24–26
dyeing **2**:16, **9**:*63*
dysentery **3**:33

E

Edessa, County of **3**:12, 19, **10**:28
education **3**:*39–44*, **10**:30
    Charlemagne's educational reforms **2**:36–37, **3**:39
    of children **2**:39–40, 42
    humanism and **5**:*8*, 9
    in India **5**:25
    Islamic **3**:*43–44*, **7**:36
    in Korea **6**:17
    medical schools **4**:68, **6**:64
    in monasteries **3**:39–40, **7**:22, **8**:64
    musical **7**:39
    See also apprentices; universities
Edward I, *king of England* **1**:23, 2:20, **3**:*45*, 54, *64*, 68, **5**:34, 65, **8**:15–16, **9**:*25*, **10**:*47–48*
Edward II, *king of England* **3**:54, **9**:*25*
Edward III, *king of England* **3**:54, **5**:10, *11*, 12, *18*, **6**:*41*, **7**:6
Edward IV, *king of England* **10**:55–56
Edward the Black Prince **5**:10
Edward the Confessor, *king of England* **3**:51, **6**:33, **10**:57
Egypt **3**:46–47, **6**:47–48
    Fatimid dynasty **3**:46, **8**:*42*
    Saladin **2**:10, 11, **3**:46–47, **9**:10
    See also Cairo
El Cid **9**:45
Eleanor of Aquitaine **3**:*48*, 53, 54, **10**:*62*
embroidery **3**:*49–50*, **10**:*63*
enamels, Limoges **7**:9
England **3**:51–54
    cathedrals **2**:24–28
    conversion to Christianity **1**:18–19
    language **6**:20, 25–26
    legal systems **6**:23
    literature **2**:38, **6**:25–26
    Norman conquest of **3**:50, 51–53, **6**:25, **7**:45, 47
    Parliament **3**:*45*, 54, **8**:*15–16*, **9**:58
    Plantagenet kings **1**:17
    taxes **9**:57–59

    trade with the Low Countries **6**:*38*, 40
    Viking invasion **1**:16, 19, **3**:51, **6**:33, **10**:36
    See also Anglo-Saxons; Hundred Years' War; London
entertainment *See* theater and entertainment
epics **6**:26
Erasmus, Desiderius **5**:8
Erec and Enide **6**:27
Erik the Red **3**:55, 56, **9**:15
Eriksson, Leif **3**:55, 56
"estates," three **2**:51–52, **4**:36, **8**:15
Estonia **1**:*46*, 47
Ethiopian church **3**:5
Eustace the Monk **7**:61
Eutyches **7**:51–52
Exchequer, the **3**:53
excommunication **2**:56, **4**:58
execution **3**:*10–11*, **10**:*10*, 44
exploration **1**:9, **3**:55, *56–58*, **6**:9
    See also Marco Polo
eyeglasses **10**:5
eyvans **5**:*41*

F

fables **6**:27
fabliaux **6**:27, 28
fairies **6**:43
fairs and markets **3**:*27*, 59–60, **7**:7, **4**:*15*, **9**:*67*, **10**:16
falconry **3**:*23*, **4**:*20*
famines and disasters **2**:62, **3**:*61–62*, **8**:39
    See also Black Death
farming *See* agriculture
Fatimid dynasty **2**:10–11, **3**:47
    in Egypt **3**:46, **8**:*42*
felt **9**:*62*, *63*
fencing **9**:49
Ferdinand of Aragon **9**:47
Ferdinand the Catholic **4**:39
festivals **2**:12, **3**:*25–26*, *63*, **7**:30 **10**:43
feudalism **3**:*64–68*
Fez **6**:68
fidelity **3**:67–68
fiefs **3**:64, 65–66, **6**:12, **7**:41, **8**:9, 48
Field of the Cloth of Gold **10**:*12*
field systems **1**:13–14
Fieschi family **4**:28
Firuz Shah Tughluq, *Tughluq sultan* **5**:*28*
fish **1**:15, **4**:7–8
flagellants **1**:*58*
Flanders **1**:*62*, 68, **5**:10, **6**:39–41, **9**:58
    See also Bruges; Ghent
flax **1**:14, **9**:*64*
flooding **2**:*62*, **3**:61
Florence **1**:*24*, **2**:58, 59, **4**:*4–5*, *37*, 48, **5**:53, **7**:6, *24* **8**:20, 38, **10**:*13*, 16, *46*
    See also Medici family
food and drink **3**:*23*, **4**:*6–9*, **6**:54
    crops **1**:14
    meat **1**:15, **4**:6–8, **6**:31, **10**:*42*
    peasant **3**:25
    wine **1**:14, *15*, **4**:8
fools (jesters) **9**:66
foot binding **10**:64
forests **4**:*10–11*, **5**:17–18, **7**:59
    deforestation **4**:11, **6**:52
Formigny, Battle of **5**:12
Four Books of Sentences **9**:17
France **4**:*12–15*
    Angevins **1**:*17*, **4**:13, **7**:48
    cathedrals **2**:23, *26*, *27*
    Estates General **8**:*16–17*, 20, **9**:*59*
    literature **6**:27, 28
    peasant uprisings **8**:20–21

    taxes **9**:58, 59
    See also Hundred Years' War; Low Countries; Paris
Francis I, *king of France* **10**:*12*
Francis II, *Holy Roman emperor* **4**:*52*
Francis of Assisi, St. **4**:16, *21–22*, **7**:15
Franciscans **4**:21–22, **7**:17
Franks **1**:52–53, **4**:*17–18*, 29, 66, **6**:39–40, **10**:*49*
Frederick I, "Barbarossa," *Holy Roman emperor* **3**:20, **4**:19, 64
Frederick II, *Holy Roman emperor* **3**:21, **4**:*20*, **5**:18, **6**:67–68, **10**:32
Frederick III, *Holy Roman emperor* **4**:*52*
Frederick the Wise **8**:*51*
free companies **7**:60–61
Freemasons **1**:26
freemen **2**:40, **8**:18
frescoes **7**:67
friars **2**:34, 56, **4**:16, *21–23*, **7**:21
Friars Minor **4**:16, *21–22*
friendship **6**:*37*
Frisians **6**:38–39
Froissart, Jean **4**:*62*
Fugger family **7**:11, 28, 43
Fujinara Sumitomo **7**:61
Fujiwara clan **5**:55, 56–57
Fujiwara Teika **6**:30
Funan, kingdom of **9**:38–39
funerals *See* death and burial
furniture **5**:6
Fustat, al- **2**:10–11, **3**:46

G

Galileo **1**:35, 37, **9**:23
galleys **10**:*24*
Gama, Vasco da **3**:58, **6**:9, **10**:21
gambling **3**:23
games *See* sports and games; toys and games
García I, *king of Spain* **9**:44–45
gardens **4**:*24–25*
Gardens of the Righteous (book) **5**:40
Garter, Order of the **6**:14
Gawain and the Green Knight **6**:26
Gawain-poet **6**:26
Gedi **2**:*60*
Gediminas, *grand duke of Lithuania* **1**:49
Genghis Khan **4**:26, **5**:47, **7**:29–30, **8**:25
Genoa **2**:*58*, **3**:21, **4**:27–28, 37, **5**:51, 52, **6**:67, **7**:7, **8**:*38*, **10**:35
Gentile da Fabriano **7**:68
Geoffrey of Anjou **1**:17, **6**:12
Geoffrey of Monmouth **4**:62, **6**:13
Geoffrey Plantagenet **7**:48
Geography (book) **6**:56
Germany **4**:*29–3*
    cathedrals **2**:28
    and Charlemagne **4**:29–30
    and Poland **8**:32
    towns and cities **10**:*14*, *15*
    See also Hanseatic League; Saxony
Géza, *Hungarian ruler* **5**:13
Ghana **1**:*5*, 6, **7**:12
ghanats **9**:11
Ghazali, al- **8**:55–56, **9**:18
Ghazan, Mahmud **8**:25
Ghent **6**:*41*, 52, **10**:*14*
Ghibellines **4**:4, **5**:*50*, 52, **10**:46
Ghiordes knot **2**:15, 16
Gibraltar **9**:*42*, *43*
Giotto **7**:68, **8**:*60*
glass **1**:*24*, **4**:33–34, **6**:*54*
    Islamic **5**:*42*
    stained **1**:25, **2**:*27*, *33*, **4**:*33*, 55, **8**:*66*
    See also mosaics

Glyndwr, Owain **10**:48
Godfrey of Bouillon **3**:12
gods, pagan **7**:62
gold **7**:9, 10, 12, *24*, 25, **9**:64
Golden Book **2**:58
Golden Bull **1**:60, **5**:14
Golden Horde **8**:32, **10**:29
Gothic script **10**:67
Gothic style
   cathedrals **2**:*23, 25, 26–28*, **7**:67–68, **8**:14
   painting and sculpture **7**:*64, 67–68*
Goths **4**:57
government **4**:35–37, **10**:38
   See also parliaments
grail, holy **6**:13
Granada **4**:38–39, **9**:47
Grand Ordinance (1357) **4**:37
Granson, Battle of **9**:*54*
Great Mosque *See* mosques
Great Schism (Great Western Schism; Avignon Schism) **4**:40–41, **8**:6–7, 65, **9**:5
Great Viet State **9**:40
Great Zimbabwe **1**:5, *11*
Greece **4**:42–43
Greek (language) **6**:18, 19
Greek fire **2**:6
Greenland **3**:55, **9**:15, **10**:37
Gregorian chant **7**:38
Gregory I, "the Great," *pope* **4**:*44*, 7:16, 38, **8**:4, 5, 52, *64*
   and purgatory **4**:54, **8**:63
Gregory V, *pope* **4**:*64*
Gregory VII, *pope* **4**:63, **7**:48, **8**:5, 6, 35, 64
Gregory IX, *pope* **5**:31, **6**:23, **8**:6
Gregory XI, *pope* **4**:40
Gregory XII, *pope* **4**:41
Gregory XIII, *pope* **2**:12
Gregory the Great *See* Gregory I
Gregory the Illuminator, St. **1**:29
Gregory of Tours **7**:13
Grosseteste, Robert **9**:23
Guelfs **4**:4, **5**:50, 52, **10**:46
Guesclin, Bertrand du **5**:11
Gui, Bernard **5**:32
Guide for the Perplexed (book) **6**:46
Guido d'Arezzo **7**:39
guilds **3**:26–27, **4**:45–48, **6**:53, **7**:7, 9, *64*, 66
Guillaume de Lorris **6**:28
Guiscard, Robert **7**:47–48
Guiscard, Roger **5**:51, **7**:47
gunpowder **2**:21, **9**:48–49, **10**:4, 50, 52, 53
guns **1**:33, **10**:50
   See also cannons; gunpowder
Gunthamund, *Vandal king* **1**:50
Gupta Empire **5**:24–26, **10**:33
Gutenberg, Johannes **8**:*12*

H
Haakon VI, *king of Norway* **9**:16
Hadith **5**:40
Haggadah **5**:*64*
Hagia Sophia **2**:*68*, **6**:5, **7**:57
Hakim, al-, *Fatimid caliph* **3**:47
halberds **1**:*32*
Halloween **7**:63
Hamburg **2**:59, **10**:14
handball **9**:49, 51
handwriting **10**:66–67
Hanseatic League **1**:62, **2**:59, 60, **4**:32, 49–50, **6**:34, **7**:61, **10**:20, 21
Hapsburgs **4**:51–52, *64*, **9**:53–54
harakiri **5**:56
harnesses, horse **4**:65, 66
Harold II, *king of England* **3**:51–52, **10**:*57*
Harold II Bluetooth, *king of Denmark* **9**:13, 14–15
Harsa **5**:26

Hartmann von Aue **4**:31
Harun ar-Rashid, *Abbasid ruler* **1**:40, *41*, **5**:46
Hastings, Battle of **1**:19, **7**:45, 47, **10**:49, 57
Hattin, Battle of **3**:14, 20, **9**:10
hauberks **1**:31
heating **5**:5–6
heaven and hell **4**:53–54
   See also death and burial
Hebrew **6**:19–20
Hedeby **9**:16
hegira **7**:37
Heian **5**:55
Heijo **5**:55
Helena, *Roman empress* **8**:28
Héloïse **1**:*4*
Henry I, *king of England* **3**:53
Henry I, *king of Germany* **1**:59
Henry II, *Holy Roman emperor* **8**:31
Henry II, *king of England* **1**:*17*, **3**:48, 52, 53–54, **4**:13, **5**:34, **6**:23, **7**:48, **8**:66 **10**:62
Henry III, *Holy Roman emperor* **4**:63
Henry IV, *Holy Roman emperor* **4**:63, **8**:5, *6*
Henry V, *king of England* **3**:7, **5**:11
Henry VI, *Holy Roman emperor* **3**:17
Henry VI, *king of England* **3**:54, **5**:*11*, 12, **10**:55, 56
Henry VII, *king of England* **3**:54
Henry VIII, *king of England* **10**:12
Henry the Lion **4**:50
Henry the Navigator **3**:58, **6**:56, **9**:46
Hephthalites **5**:16
Heraclius, *Byzantine emperor* **2**:5, **9**:12
heraldry **4**:55–56, **6**:13
herbal medicines **1**:58, **4**:24, **6**:63–64, **7**:22
heresy **2**:56, **3**:10, **4**:*57–60*, **5**:30–32, **6**:42, **7**:15, **10**:*9*
   See also Hus, Jan; inquisition
Hildebrand **8**:5
Hildegard of Bingen **4**:61, **7**:15
Hinduism **5**:24, **7**:14, **8**:29, *46*
History of the Kings of Britain **6**:13
history writing **4**:62
Hohenstaufen, the **5**:50
Holy Roman emperor **4**:63–64, **8**:34, 36
   and the Orthodox church **7**:49–50
   See also Charlemagne; Frederick I; Frederick II; Hapsburgs
Holy Roman Empire **2**:57–58, 59, **4**:30–32, 37, *63–64*, **8**:35, 36, 67
   See also Hapsburgs
Honorius III, *pope* **4**:20, **8**:6
horses **1**:31, **2**:65–66, **4**:*65–66*, **6**:11–12, **7**:*30*, **9**:51, **10**:22–23
   and agriculture **1**:12, **4**:65, *66*, **10**:5–6
   See also cavalry
Hospitalers (Knights Hospitaler) **3**:13, **4**:68
hospitals **4**:25, *67–68*
   See also disease
houses and homes **5**:*4–7*
   castles as **2**:22
   gardens **4**:25
   Mongol **9**:*63*
   peasant **1**:*22*, **3**:24–25, **5**:*4*
   in towns and cities **10**:15, *17*
   Viking **9**:*15*, **10**:38
   village **10**:42
   See also building techniques
Huaybiyah, Treaty of al- **7**:37
Hugh Capet **2**:14, **4**:12, **8**:13
Hugh the Great **2**:63
Hugh of Saint Victor **7**:15

Hülegü **8**:25
humanism **5**:*8–9*, **8**:58, 59
Hunayn ibn Ishaq al-Ibadi **8**:55
Hundred Years' War **3**:54, **4**:14, 62, **5**:*10–12*, **6**:4, **10**:50, 51, 52
   looting and pillaging **10**:45, 46
   and mercenary soldiers **7**:60–61
   See also Joan of Arc
Hungary **1**:45, **5**:*13–14*, **7**:55
   Magyars **5**:13, **6**:45
Hung-wu, *emperor of China* **2**:49
Huns **1**:50, **2**:29, **5**:*15–16*, **9**:31, **10**:34
hunting and falconry **3**:22–23, **4**:*11, 20*, **5**:*17–18*
Hunyadi, János **5**:14
Hus, Jan **1**:60, **4**:*57*, 60, **5**:19, **8**:66
Hussites **4**:60, **5**:19
Hywel Dda, *Welsh ruler* **10**:47

I
Ibn al-Haytham **9**:20
Ibn Battutah **3**:57, **6**:9, 56, **8**:29
Ibn Ezra, Abraham **8**:56
Ibn Fodhlan **3**:56
Ibn Gabirol, Solomon **8**:56
Ibn Khaldun **3**:*6*
Ibn Rushd *See* Averroës
Ibn Sina *See* Avicenna
Ice, Battle on the **9**:8
Iceland **8**:*17*, **9**:15, **10**:37
   sagas **10**:39
iconography and iconoclasm **2**:4, 8, **5**:*20–21*, **7**:9, 14–15, 51, 65
   Iconoclastic Controversy **2**:8, **5**:21, **7**:52
Idrisi, al- **3**:57, **6**:56
Ife, kingdom of **1**:5, *8–9*
Igor, *grand prince of Kiev* **6**:7
illumination **2**:*62*, **3**:*41*, **5**:*22–23*, 33
   Jewish **5**:*23, 62*
   See also writing
Imad ad-Din Zengi **3**:19, **10**:28
imams (mullahs) **8**:43
India **5**:*24–29*
   alphabet **10**:66
   languages **6**:18
   Tamerlane **5**:28, **7**:32, **9**:55
   universities **10**:33
inflation **7**:25–26
Innocent III, *pope* **2**:56, **3**:20, **4**:20, 21, 58, **5**:31, 65, **8**:5–6, *7*, 65
Innocent IV, *pope* **4**:23, 28, 58, **5**:32, **8**:6
Innocent VII, *pope* **4**:41
inquisition **2**:56, **4**:58, **5**:30–32, 66–67, **6**:43, **8**:66 **9**:47, **10**:*9*
   See also heresy
instruments, musical **7**:39
insurance **7**:7, **10**:20
International Gothic style **7**:68
Investiture Controversy **8**:35
Ireland **5**:*33–34*
   missionaries **7**:16
Irenaeus, St. **8**:4
Irene, *Byzantine empress* **2**:7, 8, 35, **5**:21, **7**:52
ironworking **6**:53–54, **7**:8, 12 **8**:38, **10**:*8*
Isabella of Bavaria, *queen of France* **2**:*53*
Isabella of Castile **9**:47
Isabella of France, *queen of England* **4**:13
Isidore of Seville **8**:35
Isidorian Decretals **8**:9
Islam **5**:35–40, *63*
   and the afterlife **4**:54
   and charity **2**:33
   and Jerusalem **5**:60–61
   and marriage **6**:60
   and music **7**:40
   punishment for crimes **3**:11
   and relics **8**:51
   See also Koran; Muhammad

Islamic culture **5**:*41–43*
   art and architecture **5**:*7, 42–43*
   dress **3**:36
   education **3**:43–44, **7**:36
   furnishings **5**:6
   gardens **4**:25
   glass **4**:34
   houses **5**:*6–7*
   illuminated books **5**:*23*
   language **6**:20
   merchants **3**:56, **7**:6, **10**:21
   mosaics **7**:*34*
   pottery **8**:41–42
   public baths **5**:5
   slaves **9**:32
   town life **3**:24
   trade **5**:47, **10**:*18*, 19
   women **10**:64
   wrestling **9**:50
   See also Koran; mosques
Islamic Empire **5**:*44–47*
   in Africa **1**:6, 7–8, 10–11, **2**:60, **6**:8, 68
   Egypt **3**:46–47
   Granada **4**:38–39
   India **5**:26–29
   Jerusalem **5**:*60–61*, **9**:10
   Jews in Muslim lands **5**:63
   in the Mediterranean **6**:66–67
   Persia **8**:23–24
   Sicily **5**:50, 51
   Spain **6**:24, **9**:42–43
   towns and cities **10**:13, 15
   See also Abbasid dynasty; Ottoman Empire; Seljuk Turks; Umayyad dynasty
Islamic scholarship **1**:*36*, **4**:62, 68, **5**:48, **6**:29–30, **8**:54–56, **9**:18, **10**:33
   See also Averroës; Avicenna
Istanbul *See* Constantinople
Italy **5**:*49–53*
   cathedrals **2**:28
   communes and city-states **2**:57–59, **4**:37, 46, **5**:*51–52*, **10**:14–15
   earthquake **3**:62
   literature **6**:28–29
   town houses **10**:17
   See also Florence; Genoa; Milan; Papal States; Pisa; Sicily; Siena; Venice
Ivan I, *grand duke of Moscow* **9**:8
Ivan III, "the Great," *Russian prince* **9**:9
Ivan Asen, *czar of Bulgaria* **1**:44

J
Jacquerie revolt **8**:21
Jadwiga, *queen of Poland* **8**:32, **9**:37
Jagiello, *king of Poland and Lithuania* **1**:48, 49, **8**:32, **9**:37
Jagiellonian dynasty **1**:48
Jalal ad-Din ar-Rumi **5**:38
James I, *king of Scotland* **10**:10
James the Great, St. **8**:28, **9**:43–44
Jani Beg **9**:9
Janissaries **7**:57, **9**:33
Japan **5**:*54–59*
   clothing **3**:38
   furnishings **5**:6
   gardens **4**:25
   Heian period **3**:38, **5**:55–56, *57*, **7**:44
   heraldry **4**:56
   houses **5**:7
   Kamakura period **3**:38
   Kofun period **5**:55
   legal codes **6**:24
   literature **5**:57, **6**:30
   monasteries **4**:25
   Mongol invasions **5**:58, **10**:54
   nobility **7**:44
   pirates **7**:61
   religion **5**:55, 56

SET INDEX

samurai 3:38, 4:56, 5:56, 57, 6:24, 7:44
   shoguns 5:54, 57–59, 6:24, 7:44
   Sumo wrestling 9:50
   writing 6:30
Java 9:41
Jayavarman II, *Khmer king* 9:39
Jean de Meun 6:28
Jerome, St. 6:19, 10:68
Jerusalem 3:12, 13, 16, 17,19, 4:68, 5:60–61, 8:28, 52, 9:10
   Kingdom of 3:12, 19
   Wailing Wall 5:61, 66
   See also Crusades
jesters 9:66
jewelry 1:53, 3:37, 7:9, 9:35, 10:38, 39
Jews and Judaism 5:40, 62–67
   and anti-Semitism 5:62, 64–65, 10:46
   books 5:63, 64
   dress 3:36
   illuminated manuscripts 5:23, 62
   in Istanbul 7:57
   and Jerusalem 5:60, 61
   moneylenders 7:26
   philosophy 8:56–57
   priests 8:43
   in Spain 6:24, 9:46–47
   synagogues 1:23
   See also Maimonides
Jimmu Tenno, *emperor of Japan* 5:54–55
Joachim of Fiore 7:15
Joan of Arc 5:12, 68, 7:15
John I, *king of England* 1:17, 2:56, 3:54, 6:33
   See also Magna Carta
John I, *king of Portugal* 10:61
John II Comnenus, *Byzantine emperor* 8:33
John II, *king of France* 5:11, 6:14, 8:20
John II, *king of Portugal* 1:9
John VIII, *pope* 8:5
John XII, *pope* 4:63
John XV, *pope* 7:13
John XXIII, *antipope* 4:41
John de Baliol 9:25
John of Damascus, St. 7:50, 52
John of Gaunt, *duke of Lancaster* 4:60
John of Luxembourg, *king of Bohemia* 1:60
John of Montecorvena 7:17
John of Salisbury 8:35
jongleurs 3:7, 7:40
journeymen 4:46
jousting *See* tournaments and jousts
Joyeuse Entrée, La 6:40
Judah ha-Levi 8:56
Justin I, *Byzantine emperor* 6:4, 9:63
Justinian I, *Byzantine emperor* 2:5, 68, 6:4–5
   legal system 6:4, 21, 22, 23
Jutes 1:52

K

Kaaba 1:21, 6:61, 62, 8:29
Kaifeng 2:49, 3:26
Kallinikos 2:6
Kalmar, Union of 9:16
Kammu, *emperor of Japan* 5:55
Kanauj 5:26
Kao Tsung, *emperor of China* 2:46
Karakorum 7:31, 32
Karle, Guillaume 8:21
Kazakh nomads 2:30
Kenneth MacAlpin 9:24
Khazars 2:30, 6:44
Khmer Empire 9:39
Khosrow I, *Sassanid king* 8:22, 25, 9:11–12
Khosrow II, *Sassanid king* 9:12

Khwarezm 7:29
Khwarizmi, al- 5:48, 9:20
Kiev 6:6–7, 44, 8:32, 9:6–7, 10:37
Kievan Rus 6:7, 9:6–7
Kilwa 1:5, 6:8–9
Kindi, al- 5:48, 8:55
kings 4:36, 8:34–35, 36
Kipchak 10:29
Ki Tsurayuki 6:30
knights 2:40, 51–52, 4:66, 6:10–14, 36, 7:41, 10:11–12, 49
   See also chivalry; samurai; Teutonic knights; tournaments and jousts
Knights Hospitaler *See* Hospitalers
Knights of Saint John 2:17
Knights Templar *See* Templars
knörrs 9:26, 27
Kokinshu 6:30
Kongo 1:9
Konrad von Marburg 5:32
Konya 10:27
Koran 5:23, 35–36, 41, 6:20, 10:68
   See also Islam
Korea 6:15–17, 9:33
Koryo 6:16–17
Kosovo, Battle of 7:55
Kotuz, *ruler of Egypt* 6:47
Krak des Chevaliers 2:17, 21, 3:15
Kraków 8:31
Kublai Khan 2:49, 4:22, 5:58, 6:57, 7:17, 27, 31–32, 9:59
Kufic script 10:68
Kulikovo, Battle of 9:9
Kumans (Kipchak) 10:29

L

Ladino 5:67
Ladislas I, *king of Hungary* 5:14
Lalibela, *king of Ethiopia* 3:5
Lancelot 6:27
land *See* property and land
Langton, Stephen 2:56
language 6:18–20
   Arabic 5:41, 48, 6:19–20, 29
   Asian 6:20
   Coptic 3:4
   in Europe 6:18–19, 20
   Jewish 5:67
   See also Latin; writing
Languedoc, tax riots 9:58
las Casas, Bartolomé de 4:22
Las Navas de Tolosa, Battle of 9:45
last rites 8:45
Lateran Council, Fourth 8:6
Latin 3:39–40, 6:18, 19, 8:67–68, 10:68
Latin states *See* Crusader states
Latvia 1:47
law and legal codes 3:53, 6:4, 21–24, 8:48
lead 7:10, 12
Leaning Tower of Pisa 2:24
Lechfeld, Battle of 5:13, 6:45, 10:49
Legnano, Battle of 4:19
Leo I, *pope* 5:16, 8:4
Leo I, *Byzantine emperor* 2:8, 5:21, 7:52
Leo III, *pope* 2:35–36, 4:63, 5:51, 8:64, 65
Leo IV, *Byzantine emperor* 2:7
Leo V, *Byzantine emperor* 2:8
Leo VI, *Byzantine emperor* 6:59
León 9:44–45
Leonardo da Vinci 8:60, 10:8
Leopold V, *duke of Austria* 3:17
leprosy and lepers 3:34, 4:45, 67, 68, 7:59
libraries, Islamic 5:48, 10:33
life, elixir of 9:21
life expectancy 3:24
light, study of 9:20, 23
Limoges, enamels 7:9
Lincoln Cathedral 2:26–27

Lindisfarne 10:36
Lindisfarne Gospels 5:22
linen 1:14, 9:64
Li Po 6:30
literature 6:25–30
   Chaucer, Geoffrey 2:38
   Christine de Pisan 2:53
   and courtly love 3:6, 7
   and the Crusades 3:21
   Dante 3:30, 4:54, 6:28–29
   Islamic 5:43
   Japanese 5:57, 6:30
   ministerial poets 4:31
   poems of Rumi 5:38
   Song of Roland 2:37, 6:11, 26
   See also history writing
Lithuania 1:47, 48–49, 8:32, 9:37, 61
Little Armenia 1:29
Little Ice Age 2:62, 3:61
livery companies 7:7
livestock 1:15, 6:31–32
Llywelyn ap Gruffudd 3:45, 10:47
Lollards 6:19
Lombard League 4:19
Lombard, Peter *See* Peter Lombard
Lombards 1:53, 5:49, 50–51, 8:8, 10:34
   and Gregory the Great 4:44
London 3:61, 4:36, 6:33–34, 54
longbows 1:32–33, 5:11–12, 9:48, 10:50
looms 2:15, 16, 6:52, 53, 9:62
Lord of Misrule 3:63
Lorenzetti, Ambrogio 5:49, 53
Lothair I, *king of France* 5:51
Louis I, *king of Hungary* 5:14, 8:32
Louis VI, *king of France* 4:13
Louis VII, *king of France* 3:19–20, 48, 4:13, 10:62
Louis VIII, *king of France* 4:68
Louis IX, *king of France* 2:14, 64, 4:14, 6:35, 8:52
Louis XI, *king of France* 1:68
Louis the Pious, *Holy Roman emperor* 4:30
love and friendship 6:36–37
   See also chivalry; courtly love
Low Countries 6:38–41, 10:23
   See also Bruges; Flanders
Lübeck 2:59, 4:49, 50, 10:14
Lucius III, *pope* 4:58, 59
Lull, Ramón (Raymond) 2:52, 7:17
luster 4:34, 8:42
Luxembourg, House of 1:60

M

MacMurrough, Dermot *king of Ireland* 5:34
madrasahs 3:44, 46, 7:36
Madurai Temple 5:27
magic and superstition 4:10, 6:42–43, 10:61
Magna Carta 3:54, 4:35
Magyars 2:30, 5:13, 6:44–45, 9:36
Mahdali dynasty 6:8, 9
Mahmud of Ghazna, "Sword of Islam" 5:26, 8:24
Maimonides (Moses ben Maimon) 5:63, 67, 6:46, 65, 8:56
Malachy I, *king of Ireland* 5:34
Mali 1:5, 6–8, 10:33
Malik as-Salih Ayyub, al- 6:47
Malik Shah, *Seljuk sultan* 10:26–28
Malinke people 1:6–7
Malleus Maleficarum (book) 10:59
malnutrition 3:33, 62
Malory, Sir Thomas 6:25, 28
Malta 6:68
Mamluks 2:11, 3:5, 15, 21, 29, 47, 6:47–48, 62, 7:58, 9:33
Mamun, al- 1:40, 8:55
Mani 6:49–50
Manichaeanism 6:49–50

manorial system 3:65
manufacturing 6:51–54
   See also guilds; mining; textiles
manuscripts, illuminated *See* illumination
Man'yoshu 5:57
Manzikert, Battle of 1:44, 2:9, 30, 3:17, 10:26
Mappa Mundi (map) 6:55
maps and mapmakers 3:57, 6:55–56
Marcel, Etienne 8:20, 21
Marco Polo 2:31, 66, 3:58, 6:57, 7:6, 27, 9:28
Margaret I, *queen of Denmark, Norway, and Sweden* 9:16
Marguerite of Burgundy 4:68
Marie de France 6:27
Marienburg 9:60, 61
markets *See* fairs and markets
Mark, St. 3:4
marriage 2:40, 6:36, 58–60, 10:59–60, 64
Marriage of the Arnolfini, The (painting) 3:37
Martel, Charles 4:18
martial arts, Korean 6:15, 16
Martin IV, *pope* 5:52
Martin V, *pope* 4:41, 8:7
Martin of Tours, St. 7:19, 20
Martini, Simone 7:68
Mary of Burgundy 4:52, 6:41
Mary, Virgin 10:59
masons 1:25–26, 64, 65
Masudi, al- 6:9
Mataram kingdom 9:41
mathematics 5:48
Matilda (the Empress Maud) 1:17, 3:52
Matilda of Tuscany 4:4
Maximilian I, *Holy Roman emperor* 4:52, 6:41
meat 1:15, 4:6–8, 6:31, 10:42
Mecca 1:21, 5:37, 6:61–62, 7:37, 58, 8:29
Medici family 2:59, 4:5, 5:53, 7:26, 28, 43, 10:15
medicine 6:63–65
   herbal 1:58, 4:24, 6:63–64, 7:22
   and Hildegard of Bingen 4:61
   Islamic 4:68, 5:48
   medical schools 4:68, 6:64
   operations 4:68, 6:64
   See also Avicenna; Maimonides
Medina 1:21, 6:62, 7:37
Mediterranean 6:66–68, 10:21
Mehmed II, *Ottoman sultan* 5:47, 7:4, 55, 56, 58, 10:29
mendicants 4:21–23
merchants 2:13, 3:40, 56, 6:51, 7:5–7, 24–25, 27–28, 10:18–19, 20, 21
   See also guilds; trade
Mercia 3:51
Merovingians 4:17–18
Messina 5:50
metalwork 1:53, 3:29, 6:53–54, 7:8–9, 8:38, 10:8, 39
   See also arms and armor; mining
Methodius *See* Cyril and Methodius
Michelangelo 8:60, 9:30
Middle East
   Islamic Empire in 5:45–46
   population 8:37
   postal services 2:66, 5:45
Middle English 6:20, 25–26
midwives 10:61
Mieszko I, *king of Poland* 8:31, 9:36
migration 8:39
Milan 2:58, 59, 4:37, 5:53, 10:14
mills 10:6–7, 41–42
Minakshi 5:27
Minamoto clan 5:55, 57
Minamoto Tomoe 5:56
Minamoto Yoritomo 5:57–58

Minamoto Yoshiie 7:*44*
Mindaugas 1:*48–49*
mining 7:*10–12*
ministerials 4:31
minstrels 3:7, 23
mints (coin workshops) 7:24
miracles and mysticism 7:*13–15*, 8:52, 66
    visions of Hildegard of Bingen 4:*61*, 7:15
    See also relics
missionaries 7:*16–17*
Mocenigo, Giovanni 4:*37*
Model Parliament 3:45, 54, 8:*15–16*
Mohammad *See* Muhammad
Mombasa 1:5
monasteries 2:56, 7:*18–22*
    books copied 8:10
    Buddhist 7:22
    Cluniac 1:68
    farming 7:22, 10:*6–7*
    gardens 4:24, *25*
    Greek 4:43
    and hospitals/medicine 4:67–68, 7:22
    and illuminated manuscripts 5:22, *23*
    Irish 5:33, 6:19
    Japanese 4:25
    Orthodox 7:*50*
    schools and learning 3:39–40, 7:22, 8:64, *67–68*
    See also Benedictines; Carthusians; Cistercians; convents
monasticism 7:19–20
money 7:*23–28*, 8:49
    See also taxes
moneylenders 7:25, *26*
Mongols 2:30, 66, 3:21, 5:47, 6:48, 7:*29–32*, 9:*63*
    and China 2:49, 50, 4:26, 7:5, *29*, 31–32, 9:*55*
    horses 4:*65*, 7:*30*, 10:*50*
    invasions 1:29, 5:14, *58*, 6:17, 8:25, 32, 9:*7–8*, 9, 10:54
    See also Genghis Khan; Kublai Khan; Tamerlane
monks 7:20
    See also Benedictines; Carthusians; Cistercians
Monophysitism 3:4, 7:51–52
Monte Cassino 1:*54*
Montfort, Simon de 3:45, 8:15
Moors 4:38, 9:*43*
Moravians 6:45
Morgarten, Battle of 9:*53*
mosaics 2:58, 7:*33–34*
Moscow 7:*53*, 9:*8–9*, *34*
Moses ben Maimon *See* Maimonides
Moses ben Nahman 8:57
mosques 5:*41*, *47*, 7:*35–36*
    at Cairo 3:*46*, 7:*35*, 36
    at Kilwa 6:*8*
    Friday 5:*41*, 7:35–36
    Great Mosque at Damascus 3:*28–29*, 5:*42*, *46*, 7:36
    in Istanbul 7:*58*
motte and bailey castles 2:*18–19*
Mu'awiyah, *Umayyad caliph* 3:28
Muhammad 1:*21*, 4:*54*, 5:35, *37*, 5:60, *61*, 6:61–62, 7:*37*, 10:*64*
    See also Islam
Muhammad I, *Nasrid ruler* 4:38
Muhammad V, *Nasrid ruler* 4:39
Muhammad XI, *Nasrid ruler* 4:39
Muhammad Askia 1:8
Muhammad of Ghur 5:27
Muhammad ibn Tughluq, *sultan of Delhi* 5:28, 46
mullahs 8:43
Muqaddimah (book) 4:62
Murad I, *Ottoman sultan* 7:55
Murad II, *Ottoman sultan* 7:55, 57
Murano, glassmakers 4:*34*, 6:54

Murasaki Shikibu 5:57
Musa, Mansa 1:*7–8*
music 3:23, 7:*38–40*, 9:*67*
Muslims *See* Islam; Islamic culture; Islamic Empire; Islamic scholarship
mystery plays 3:27, 9:*65*, 66–67
mysticism *See* miracles and mysticism

N

Naadam festival 7:*30*
Nasir, al-Malik an- 6:48
Nasrid dynasty 4:38–39
Navarre 9:45, *47*
navigation 3:58, 9:28, 10:24
Nawawi 5:40
neo-Manicheans 6:50
Nestorian church 7:17, 52
Nestorius 7:51, 52
Netherlands 6:39
Neville's Cross, Battle of 9:*24*
Nicephorus I, *Byzantine emperor* 1:43
Nicholas I, *pope* 7:52, 8:5
Nicholas V, *pope* 8:8
Nicholas of Cusa 1:37
Nicopolis, Battle of 7:55
Nika Revolt 6:5
Nizam al-Mulk, *Seljuk vizier* 10:27
nobility 7:*41–44*
    children 2:40–41
    coats of arms 4:56
    and courtly love 3:6–7
    daily life 3:*22–24*, 7:*42*
    education 3:41
    and feudalism 3:66
    gardens 4:25
    houses 5:5
    hunting and falconry 5:*17*, 18
    kings and the 8:36
    in Korea 6:15, 16
    and Magna Carta 4:35
    marriage 6:58, *59*, 10:*60*
    private chaplains 8:44
    women 3:*23*, 24, 8:50, 10:*61–62*, 64
Noh plays 5:57, 9:*67*
nomads
    Arab 1:*20*, 5:*44*, 45
    steppe 2:*29–30*
Normans 2:*18–19*, 3:50, 51–53, 6:*25*, *66*, 7:*45–48*c 51–53, 9:*24–25*,10:47
Northern Crusade 9:60
Northumbria 3:51
Norway 9:13–14, *16*
notaries 10:66
Notre Dame de Paris 2:26, 8:*13*, 14
Novgorod 2:50, 60, 9:*6*, *7*, 8, 9
numerals, Arabic 9:20
Nur ad-Din Zengi 3:29, 10:28
Nuremberg 4:*32*

O

oaths, of fidelity 3:68
Odoacer 1:51, 8:68
Offa's Dyke 10:47, *48*
Ögödei 10:31
Omar Khayyam 8:24
Opus Angelicanum 3:49
ordeal, trial by 6:22
Oresme, Nicholas 1:37
Orhan, *Ottoman sultan* 7:54
Orthodox church 2:*7–8*, 7:*49–53*
    monasteries 7:19–20
    mysticism 7:14–15
    priests and clergy 8:46
    and the Roman Catholic Church 2:7–8, 7:52–53, 8:63
    split within 3:4, 7:51–52
    See also iconography and iconoclasm
Osman I, *Ottoman sultan* 7:54, 10:28
Ostrogoths 1:51, 5:15, 49

Otakar I, *king of Bohemia* 1:60
Otakar II, *king of Bohemia* 1:60, 4:51
Otto I, "the Great," *Holy Roman emperor* 4:30, *63*, 5:51, 6:45
Otto III, *Holy Roman emperor* 4:64, 8:31
Otto IV, *Holy Roman emperor* 4:20
Ottoman Empire 1:45, 2:9, 21, *67*, 68, 5:47, 6:48, 7:4, *54–58*, 10:28–29
    See also Mehmed II
outcasts 7:*59–61*
    See also leprosy and lepers
outlaws 7:59–60
Outremer 3:*12–13*, 14
Oxford University 3:41, 10:*30*, 33

P

Pachomius, St. 7:19, 20
Paciolo, Luca 7:27
paganism 7:*62–63*c, 10:*37*
pages 2:40, *51*, 3:41
painting and sculpture 4:5, *48*, 7:*64–68*, 9:*12*
    See also arts and crafts; iconography and iconoclasm; illumination; mosaics; Renaissance
Palamas, St. Gregory 7:50
Palermo 5:51, 6:*66*, 7:48
Pandyan kingdom 5:27
papacy 2:55, 8:*4–7*, 35, 36
    Charlemagne and the 2:35–36, 5:50–51
    Great Schism 4:*40–41*, 8:6–7
    and the Holy Roman Empire 2:57–58, 4:63–64
    and Rome 5:50–51, 9:5
    See also Papal States
Papal States 4:18, 5:50, 53, 8:4, *8–9*
paper and printing 2:48, 3:41, 5:9, 6:17, 8:*10–12*, 10:8
    See also illumination
Parantaka I, *Cola king* 5:26
Paris 2:26, 3:*27*, 41,4:*15*, 36, *67*, 7:11 8:*13–14*, 38, 39, 9:*58*, 10:14, 33, 38
parishes 8:64, 10:40
parliaments 3:45, 54, 8:*15–17*, 9:58
Parsees 8:23
Parzival 6:28
patriarchs 2:54, 55
Patrick, St. 5:33, 34, 7:16
Paulicians 6:50
Paul of Tarsus 8:57
Pearl 6:26
peasants 8:*18–19*, *48*, *49*
    and the Black Death 1:58
    children 2:42, 8:19
    Chinese 8:*19*
    daily life 3:*24–25*
    dress 3:*36*
    homes 1:*22*, 3:*24–25*, 5:*4*
    and money 7:25
    taxes 8:21, 9:*56–57*
    uprisings 3:54, 8:*20–21*
    women 3:25, 8:19, 10:*58–59*, *62*
    See also serfs
Peasants' Crusade 3:18
Peasants' Revolt 3:54, 8:*21*, 9:59, 10:*7*
Pechenegs 2:30, 5:13, 6:*6*, 44, 45
Pedro III, *king of Sicily* 5:52
Pelagians 4:58
Pelayo 9:43
Perfects 4:58
Periplus (manuscript) 6:8
Persia 5:44, 8:*22–25*, 4:*7*
    See also Manicheanism; Sassanid Empire
Peter III, *king of Aragon* 6:*23–24*
Peter the Hermit 3:18
Peter Lombard 8:44, 58, 9:17

Peter, St. 8:*4*, 62
Petrarch 5:8, *9*, 6:*28–29*
Philip II, *king of Spain* 2:19
Philip II Augustus, *king of France* 1:17, 2:14, 3:17, 20, 4:*12*, 14, 5:*30*, 7:48, 8:13–14, 10:*33*
Philip IV, "the Fair," *king of France* 1:62, 2:*14*, 3:10, 13, *64*, 4:14–15, 40, 6:40, 8:*7*, 16, *26*
Philip VI (Philip of Valois), *king of France* 4:13, 5:10
Philip the Bold, *duke of Burgundy* 1:68
Philip of Commynes 4:62
Philip of Swabia, *king of Germany* 4:20
Philosopher's Stone 9:21
Physica (book) 4:61
Picts 9:24
Pied Piper of Hamelin 3:62
pigs 1:15, 6:*31*, 10:*42*
pikes 10:50
pilgrimages 2:65, 3:*53*, 5:61, 6:62, 8:*27–30*, 52, 9:5, 44, 10:22, 23
Pillow Book 5:57
Pippin III, *king of the Franks* 2:35, 4:*17*, 18, 5:50, 8:4
Pippin, Donation of 8:8
piracy 7:*61*, 9:33
Pisa 2:24, 58, 3:*27*, 3:21, 5:*52* 6:*67*
Pius II, *pope* 3:*49*, 8:*7*
plague *See* Black Death
plainsong (plainchant) 7:38
Plantagenet kings 1:17
plows 1:*12*, 4:*65*, *66*, 8:*18*, 19, *47*, 10:*4*, *5–6*
poaching 4:11, 7:59
pogroms 5:65
Poitiers, Battle of 5:*10*, 11, 8:*51*
Poland 8:*31–32*, 9:36, *37*
Polanians (Polanie) 8:31
Policraticus (book) 8:35
political thought 8:*33–36*
pollution 6:54, 10:8, 16
Polo, Marco *See* Marco Polo
Polycarp, St., relics 8:51–52
Poor Clares 10:*60*
Poor Men of Lyons 4:59
popes *See* papacy
population 2:61, 8:*37–39*
    Domesday Book 3:53, 8:*38*
porcelain 8:40
portolans 6:56
Portugal 3:57, 9:46
postal services 2:66, 5:45
pottery 2:31, 45, 50, 8:*40–42*
Prague 1:59, 60 2:13, 5:*63*
Prague, Compacta of 1:60
presbyters 2:54, 8:44
Prester John 1:9, 3:5
priests and clergy 8:*43–46*
    See also bishops; monasteries
Primary Chronicle 6:6, *7*
primogeniture 7:42
printing *See* paper and printing
prisons 3:10
property and land 8:*47–50*, 10:40
    and fiefdom 3:64, 65–66, 6:12, 7:41
    land clearance 1:13
Prussia, and the Teutonic Knights 1:*47–48*, 9:60
psalters 5:23
Ptolemy of Alexandria 1:*34–37*, 6:55, *56*
punctuation 10:*67–68*
purgatory 3:31, 4:54, 8:63

Q

Qahirah, al- *See* Cairo
quadrants 1:*37*
Quaresima 10:9
quarrying, stone 7:11
Quest of the Holy Grail (book) 6:13
Qutb-ud-Din 5:*27–28*

R

rabbis **8**:43
Rajendra I, *Indian king* **9**:41
Ramayana (poem) **5**:24
Raphael **8**:59, 60
Ravenna **1**:*51*, **2**:*8*, **7**:33–34
Razi, al- **4**:68
Reims Cathedral **2**:*26*, **7**:67–68
relics **7**:13–14, **8**:*27*, *51–52*
religion
    in China **2**:45, 48
    in Japan **5**:55, 56
    See also Buddhism; church, Christian; Islam; magic and superstition; Manicheanism
religious thought and philosophy **8**:53–58
    and Averroës **1**:38
    and Avicenna **1**:39
    Jewish **6**:46
    and the universe **1**:34–35
    See also humanism; scholasticism; Thomas Aquinas
Renaissance **7**:68, **8**:59–60, 68
    and Florence **4**:5, **5**:53
Rhazes **6**:65
rice **1**:*14*, **2**:*43*, 48, **4**:9
Richard I, "the Lionheart," *king of England* **1**:17, **2**:19, **3**:7, *17*, 20, 54, **9**:10, **10**:44
Richard II, *king of England* **3**:54, **4**:*35*, **5**:*33*, **7**:*67*, **8**:21
Richard III, *king of England* **1**:17, **3**:54
Richard the Justician **1**:67
Rihlah (book) **3**:57
robbery **7**:59–60
Robert the Bruce **3**:45, **9**:25
Robert Guiscard (Robert the Cunning) **7**:47–48
Robin Hood **7**:*60*, **9**:49
Roderick, *Visigothic king* **9**:42
Roger I (Roger Guiscard) **5**:51, **7**:47
Roger II, *king of Sicily* **5**:51, **7**:*46*, 48, **8**:*61*
Roland **2**:*37*, **10**:49
Rollo, *duke of Normandy* **7**:46
Roman Catholic church **8**:62–66
    Mass **3**:*27*, **7**:14, 38, **8**:*63*, 64
    mysticism **7**:15
    and the Orthodox church **2**:7–8, **7**:52–53, **8**:63
    priests and clergy **8**:44–45
    relics **8**:52
    saints **7**:13
    See also church, Christian; friars; heresy; inquisition; missionaries; monasteries; papacy; priests and clergy; Thomas Aquinas
Romance of the Rose (poem) **3**:*22*, **6**:28, 37
romances (stories) **6**:27
Roman Empire **8**:67–68
    building techniques **1**:*63*, 66
    drama **9**:65–66
    Eastern *See* Byzantine Empire
    the emperor **8**:33
    legal system **6**:21
    and the papacy **1**:4, **8**:67
Romanesque style **8**:68
    churches and cathedrals **2**:24–*26*, **7**:48
    painting and sculpture **7**:66–67
Romanus Diogenes, *Byzantine emperor* **10**:26
Rome **5**:50–51, **9**:*4*–5, **8**:*8*, **10**:13
Romulus Augustulus **1**:*51*, **8**:68
Roses, Wars of the *See* Wars of the Roses
Rouen, tax riots **9**:58
Rua, *king of the Huns* **5**:15
Rudolf I, *Holy Roman emperor* **4**:51, 64
Rudolf IV, *duke of Austria* **4**:52
Rumi, Jalal ad-Din ar- **5**:38
Rum, Sultanate of **10**:*27*, 28
runes **9**:*13*, **10**:39
Russia **9**:6–9
    Kievan Rus **6**:*7*, **9**:6–7
    Novgorod **2**:59–60, **9**:*6*, 7, 8, 9
    and the Orthodox church **7**:*53*, 9:36
    slaves **9**:33

S

Sa'aida ben Joseph **8**:56
sacraments **8**:44
saddles, war **4**:66
Saint Albans, Battle of **10**:55
St. Anthony's fire **3**:34
St. Basil's Cathedral **7**:*53*
St. Mark's Basilica **2**:*58*, **10**:*35*
St. Peter's Basilica **8**:*8*
saints **7**:13
Saladin **2**:*10*, *11*, **3**:5, *14*–15, *20*, *46*–47, **5**:*61*, **6**:46, **9**:*10*, **10**:28
Salic Law **4**:13
Salih Ayyub, as- **6**:47
Salisbury Cathedral **2**:*28*
salt **7**:10, *12*, 23, **9**:59
Samanids **8**:24
Samarkand **9**:55
Samarra **10**:15
Samuel, *czar of Macedonia* **1**:43–44
samurai **3**:38, **4**:*56*, **5**:*56*, 57, **6**:24, *7*:44
Sancho III, *Spanish king* **9**:44, 45
San Gimignano **10**:*46*
sanitation **5**:5, **10**:16–17, 43
Sanskrit **6**:20
Santiago de Compostela **8**:*27*, 28, *52*, **9**:43–44
Saracens, pirates **7**:61
Sardinia **6**:68
Sassanid Empire **1**:*28*, **5**:44, **8**:*22*–23, *25*, **9**:*11*–12
Savonarola, Girolamo **4**:*59*, **8**:7
Saxons **1**:*52*
Saxony **1**:*59*, **4**:29, 32
Sayf ad-Din Ghazi I **10**:*28*
Sayings of the Pope **8**:5
Scandinavia **9**:13–16
    See also Vikings
scholasticism 39, **8**:57–58, 66, **9**:*17–18*
    See also Abelard, Averroës; Thomas Aquinas
schools *See* education
science and mathematics **9**:*19–23*
    and Hildegard of Bingen **4**:61
    and philosophy **8**:53, 54
    See also alchemy; astronomy; tools and technology
Scivias (book) **4**:*61*
Scotland **9**:24–25
scribes **10**:*66*, 67
scriptoria **5**:*23*, **8**:10
sculptures **7**:66, 67–68, **8**:*60*, **9**:30
scutage **6**:13
seasons *See* climate and seasons
seder meal **5**:*62*, 64
Segovia **9**:*42*, 45
Sei Shonagon **5**:57
Selim I, "the Grim," *Ottoman sultan* **7**:58
Seljuk Turks **2**:30, **3**:*16*, *17*, **5**:41, *47*, **8**:24–25, **10**:*25*–28
    Battle of Manzikert **1**:44, **2**:*9*, 30, **3**:*17*, **10**:26
Sephardim **5**:67
serfs **2**:60, **3**:*65*, 66–67, **8**:18, **9**:31–32
Sérifontaine **3**:*23*–24
Servites **4**:21, 23
Seville **2**:*28*, **9**:46
Shafi'i, Muhammad ash- **5**:39
Shams ad-Din **5**:38
Shapur I, *king of Persia* **8**:*22*, **9**:*12*
sheep **1**:*15*, **6**:*32*
Shen Kua **9**:22
shields **1**:*32*
Shi'ites **5**:38, 39
Shinto religion **5**:55
ships and seafaring **9**:26–29, **10**:24
    Arab dhows **3**:*56*, **9**:*27*
    Byzantine war galleys **2**:*6*
    Chinese **2**:*49*, **9**:*27*–28
    maps **6**:*56*
    navigation **3**:*58*, **9**:28, **10**:24
    piracy **7**:61
    Viking **9**:26–27, **10**:*36*, 39
    Viking burial ships **3**:*32*
    warfare **5**:*12*, **10**:54
Shishman, Mikhail, *czar of Bulgaria* **1**:44
shoguns **5**:*54*, 57–59, **6**:24, **7**:44
Shotoku, *emperor of Japan* **5**:55
Sicily **5**:50, *51*, 52, **6**:67–68
    Normans in **6**:*66*, **7**:47–48
    See also Roger II
sieges **2**:*21*, **10**:*53*
Siena **1**:*24*, **2**:*57*, **3**:*63*, **4**:*37*, **5**:*53*, **9**:51
Siger of Brabant **8**:*58*, **9**:18
Sigismund, *Holy Roman emperor* **1**:*60*, **5**:19, **6**:*12*
Silence, Tower of **8**:*23*
silk **2**:*7*, **9**:62–63, *64*
Silk Road **3**:*47*, 45, **10**:19
Silla **6**:15–16
silver **7**:9, 10, 11–*12*, **9**:*64*
Simeon I, *Bulgarian czar* **1**:43
Simeon Stylites, St. **7**:19
Sinai, Mt., monastery **7**:*20*
Sistine Chapel **8**:*60*, *62*
Six Authentic Compilations, The **5**:40
Sixtus IV, *pope* **8**:*7*, 62
slaves and slavery **5**:*42*, 46, **9**:30–33
    See also serfs
Slavic peoples **1**:42–43, **2**:36, **4**:31–32, **7**:*17*, *52*, **9**:34–37
    See also Balkans; Bulgars; Poland; Russia
Sluys, Battle of **5**:10, *12*, **10**:54
soccer **3**:*26*, **9**:50
society, three estates **2**:51–52, **4**:*36*, **8**:15
soldiers **6**:*14*
    free companies **7**:60–61
    Mongol armies **7**:29–31
    Seljuk **10**:*25*
    slave **9**:33
    Swiss infantry **9**:*54*
    See also knights
Solomon ben Abraham **8**:57
Solomon ben Isaac **8**:56
Solomonids **1**:10
Song of the Cid, The (poem) **6**:26
Songhai people **1**:*8*
Song of the Nibelungs, The (poem) **6**:26
Song of Roland (poem) **2**:*37*, **6**:11, 26
Soninke people **1**:6
Sonni Ali, *Songhai leader* **1**:8
souks **3**:*24*, *60*
Southeast Asia **9**:38–41
Spain *See* Spanish kingdoms
Spanish Inquisition **5**:*32*, **9**:47, **10**:*9*
Spanish kingdoms **9**:42–47
    Alhambra palace **5**:*7*, *43*
    cathedrals **2**:*28*
    Jews **5**:*63*, 66–67
    legal codes **6**:24
    literature **6**:26
    parliaments **8**:17
    pottery **8**:*42*
    See also Granada
spectacles **10**:*5*
spices **4**:8–*9*, **10**:21
spirits **6**:43
sports and games **9**:48–52
animal sports **9**:*51*, **10**:*44*
    See also hunting and falconry; toys and games
squires **2**:*40*, **3**:*41*
Srivijaya **9**:41
Stanze, the **8**:59, 60
Star, Order of the **6**:*14*
steel, Damascus **3**:29
Stefan IV Dusan, *emperor of Serbia* **1**:44–45
Stefan Nemanja, *Serbian ruler* **1**:44
Stephen, *king of England* **3**:52
Stephen I (St. Stephen), *king of Hungary* **4**:*31*, **5**:13–14
Stephen II, *king of Hungary* **5**:14
Stephen II, *pope* **5**:50, **8**:4, *8*
Stephen of Cloyes **3**:20
stirrups **4**:*66*, **10**:*49*
Stock, Simon **4**:22
stone **1**:*64*–66, **2**:19–20, **7**:11
stonemasons **4**:*48*
Straw, Jack **8**:21
Strozzi family **7**:28
studia generalia **10**:31–32
stupas **8**:*51*, 52
Sturluson, Snorri **10**:39
Suebi **1**:*51*
Sufis **5**:*38*, *39*, 43 **7**:*14*, *40*, **8**:56
Süleyman, Seljuk chieftain **10**:27
Süleyman I, "the Magnificent," *Ottoman sultan* **7**:56, *58*, **10**:29
Sumatra **9**:41
Summa Contra Gentiles (book) **9**:68
Summary of the Law **6**:46
Summa Theologiae (book) **8**:58, **9**:18, 68
sumptuary laws **7**:44
Sundiata, *Malinke king* **1**:*7*
Sunnis **5**:37–39
sunspots **1**:35
superstition *See* magic and superstition
Su Shih **2**:47
Su Sung **2**:13
Su Tung-p'o **2**:47
Svyatoslav I, *prince of Kiev* **1**:43
Swahili culture **1**:*11*, **6**:8
Sweden **9**:14
Switzerland **9**:53–54
swords **9**:48–49
Sylvester I, *pope* **8**:9
synagogues **1**:*23*

T

tabors **7**:*39*
taekwondo **6**:15, *16*
Taika Reform **5**:55
Taira clan **5**:55, 57
T'ai Tsu, *emperor of China* **8**:36
T'ai Tsung, *emperor of China* **2**:46
Takauji, *shogun of Japan* **5**:58–59
Tale of Genji, The (book) **5**:57
Tale of the Heike, The **5**:57
Tallinn **1**:*46*, *47*
Talmud **5**:*63*, 64
Tamerlane **1**:29, **3**:28, *29*, **5**:28, **6**:48, **7**:*32*, 55, **8**:*25*, **9**:55
Tannenberg, Battle of **1**:*49*, **9**:37, 61
tanneries **6**:54, **10**:8, 16
Taoism **2**:48
Tariq ibn Ziyad **9**:42
Tatars **9**:7–8
taxes and tithes **9**:56–59, **10**:41
    tithe barns **1**:*27*, **9**:*57*
    tithes **1**:27, **2**:33–34, **8**:48, **9**:57
Templars (Knights Templar) **3**:13, **8**:26
Temüjin *See* Genghis Khan
Teutonic Knights **1**:47–48, *49*, **3**:16, **4**:32, **8**:32, **9**:8, 36, 60–61
textiles **3**:*36*, **9**:62–64
    carpets and rugs **2**:15–*16*
    cloth industry **6**:51–53

damask 3:29, 36
  in Flanders 6:40
  wool 6:32, 40
  See also embroidery; wool
Thailand 9:39–40
theater and entertainment 9:65–67
  Japanese Noh plays 5:57, 9:67
  mystery plays 3:27, 9:65, 66–67
  See also dancing; music
themes (military districts) 2:5, 8
Theodora, *Byzantine empress* 6:5
Theodoric the Great, *Ostrogoth king* 1:51, 9:4
Theodosius II, *Byzantine emperor* 2:67
Thierry of Chartres 9:23
Thirteen Years' War 9:61
Thomas à Kempis 8:66
Thomas Aquinas, St. 2:33, 4:53, 8:35, 44, 66, 9:18, 68
Thousand and One Nights, The (tales) 5:42
tiles 8:41
timber 1:63–64, 6:52
Timbuktu *See* Tombouctou
tin 7:10, 12
Tiridates III, *king of Armenia* 1:28, 29
tithes *See* taxes and tithes
Toghril Beg 10:25
toilet facilities 5:5, 10:17
tolls 9:57, 10:23
Tombouctou (Timbuktu) 1:8, 10:33
Tomislav, *ruler of Croatia* 1:45
tools and technology 10:4–8
  agricultural 1:12–13, 4:65, 66, 8:18, 19, 47, 10:4, 5–6
  and horses 1:12, 4:65, 66
  ironworking 6:53–54
  for mining 7:10–11
  See also building techniques; paper and printing
Torah 5:04
torture 3:9, 10:9–10
  and the inquisition 4:58, 5:32, 66–67
Tosa Diary 6:30
tournaments and jousts 3:23, 4:56, 6:11, 10:11–12, 44
Tours, Battle of 4:18
Tower of London 6:33, 34
town halls 1:24, 61, 10:16
towns and cities 10:13–17
  populations 8:38–39
  town life 3:26–27
  See also city-states
Towton, Battle of 10:56
toys and games 2:42, 9:52
  See also sports and games
trade 10:18–21
  bills of exchange 7:5–6, 27–28, 10:20
  Byzantine 2:6–7, 10:19
  Chinese 2:45–47, 10:19
  and city-states 2:58–59, 60
  European 10:19–20, 21
  in France 4:15
  from East Africa 1:11, 6:8–9
  and guilds 4:46–47
  Islamic 5:47, 10:18, 19
  and Italy 4:34, 10:34–35
  See also fairs and markets; Hanseatic League; merchants
trade associations 7:7
transportation 2:65–66, 10:22–24
  travel hazards 10:45
  See also communications; horses; maps and mapmakers; ships and seafaring
travel *See* transportation
Travels of Marco Polo, The (book) 6:57
trebuchets 2:21
trial by ordeal 6:22, 10:9–10

Tripoli, County of (Crusader state) 3:19
troubadours 3:6, 7, 6:26, 37
Tuareg nomads 1:8
Tudors 10:56
Tu Fu 6:30
Tughluq dynasty 5:28
Turkic peoples 2:30, 5:46, 10:25–29
  See also Ottoman Empire; Seljuk Turks
Tyler, Wat 8:21

U
Uhud, Battle of 7:37
Ulfilas 1:50
Ulrich von Lichenstein 4:31
Ulugh Beg 1:36
Umayyad dynasty 1:6, 3:28, 46, 5:38, 41, 46
  art and architecture 5:43, 46
  literature 6:30
  and Persia 8:23
  trade 7:6
uncials 10:67
unicorns 6:43
universe, models of 1:34–37
universities 3:41–42, 8:14, 10:30–33
  Islamic 3:46
Urban II, *pope* 3:17–18, 8:5
Urban IV, *pope* 1:38
Urban VI, *pope*, and the Great Schism 4:40–41, 8:7

V
Vaclav I *See* Wenceslas
Valdemar II, *king of Denmark* 1:47
Vandals 1:50, 52, 6:4, 9:4, 31
Varanasi 5:29
Varangians 6:6–7, 9:6
Vasari, Giorgio 8:59
Vatican 8:59, 9:4, 5
Venice 1:44, 2:58, 66, 3:21, 4:34, 37, 5:51, 52, 53, 6:54, 67, 7:24, 34 8:38, 10:14, 17, 21, 34–35
Verdun, Treaty of (843) 4:18
Victor IV, *antipope* 4:19
vieles 7:39
Vietnamese 9:40–41
Vijayanagara 5:29
Vikings 2:61, 9:13–14, 10:36–39
  burials 3:32, 7:23
  chess set 9:52
  coins 7:23
  exploration 3:55, 56, 57
  gods 7:63, 10:37
  houses 9:15, 10:38
  invasions 1:16, 19, 3:51, 5:34, 6:33, 7:45, 9:6, 25, 10:36
  in Russia 9:6
  ships and boats 9:26–27, 10:36, 39
  warfare 10:38
village life 3:25–26, 8:48, 10:40–43
  and forests 4:11
  See also daily life
violence and threats 8:19, 10:44–46
  See also crime and punishment; outcasts; torture; warfare
"Virgin of Vladimir" (icon) 5:21
Visconti family 2:59
  Bernabo Visconti 10:9
Visigoths 1:50, 52, 53, 9:4, 42
Vladimir I, *grand prince of Kiev* 6:7, 9:6
von Eschenbach, Wolfram 4:31, 6:28
Vratislav II, *prince of Bohemia* 1:59
Vytautas, *Lithuanian leader* 1:49

W
wagons 4:65, 10:22–23
Wakefield, Battle of 10:55
Waldensians 4:58–59, 5:31

Waldo, Peter 4:58–59
Waldseemüller, Martin 6:56
Wales 10:47–48
  castles 1:23, 64, 2:20, 10:47, 48
Walid I, al- 3:28
Wallace, William 3:45, 9:25
Walter von der Vogelweide 4:31
Wang Kon 6:16–17
warfare 10:46, 49–56
  at sea 5:12, 10:54
  attacking castles 2:21
  cavalry 6:10–12, 14, 10:49
  Chinese 9:22
  horses in 4:65, 66, 6:11–12
  Islamic 5:45
  and knights 4:66, 6:13, 14, 10:49
  sieges 2:21, 10:53
  Viking 10:38
  war chronicles 4:62
  See also arms and armor; soldiers
warlocks 6:42
Wars of the Roses 3:54, 10:55–56
Warwick, Richard Neville, Earl of 10:56
watchmen, night 10:45
water 2:11, 3:33, 10:43
  See also sanitation
weapons *See* arms and armor
weaving 2:16, 6:52, 9:62
  See also looms
Welf, the 5:50
Wells Cathedral 2:24, 26–27, 28
Wenceslas, *prince of Bohemia* 1:59, 9:37
Weschler family 7:28
Wessex 3:51
Wharram Percy 10:41
White Guelfs 5:50
White Huns 5:16, 25–26
William I, "the Conqueror," *king of England* 1:19, 3:52–53, 65–66, 5:18, 7:47, 6:33, 34, 10:47, 57
  See also Domesday Book
William II, *king of England* 3:53
William III, *duke of Aquitaine* 3:7
William of Ockham 8:58, 9:18
William the Pious, *duke of Aquitaine* 2:63
Wilton Diptych 7:67
windmills 10:6, 7–8, 41
windows 2:18, 4:33, 5:4
  See also glass
wine 1:14, 15, 4:8

witchcraft 3:10, 6:42–43
Wladyslas III, *king of Poland and Hungary* 1:48
women 10:58–64
  in China 2:49, 10:64
  and Christine de Pisan 2:53
  daily life 3:25, 10:43, 58–60
  dress 3:35, 36–37
  girls 2:40, 41, 42, 3:40, 41
  Islamic 5:36
  jewelry 3:37
  and land 8:50
  in the life of a castle 2:22
  noble 3:23, 24, 8:50, 10:61–62, 64
  in the Orthodox church 8:46
  peasant 3:25, 8:19, 10:58–59, 62
  samurai 5:56
  slaves 9:33
  Viking 10:38–39
  See also courtly love; marriage
wool 6:32, 51, 52, 9:58, 62
Worms, Concordat of 8:6, 64–65
wrestling 9:50
writing 2:37, 3:39, 10:65–68
  Arabic 6:20, 10:66, 68
  Chinese 6:20, 10:65, 68
  Japanese 6:30
  See also illumination; language
Wu Hou, *empress of China* 2:46
Wycliffe, John 4:60, 5:19, 6:19, 8:66

Y
Yamato clan 5:54
Yang Ti, *Chinese emperor* 2:43–45, 10:24
Yaroslav I, *prince of Kiev* 6:6, 7
Yazdegerd II, *Sassanid king* 1:28
Yes and No (book) 1:4, 8:58, 9:17
Yi Songgye 6:17
Ypres 1:24, 6:52
Yung-lo, *emperor of China* 2:48, 50, 3:58
Yusuf I, *Nasrid ruler* 4:39
Yvain 6:27

Z
Zanzibar, slaves 9:31
Zara 3:20
Zengid Dynasty 10:28
Zeno, *Byzantine emperor* 1:51
Zizka, Jan 5:19
zodiac, signs of the 6:42, 63
Zoroastrianism 8:23

PICTURE CREDITS

Cover AKG London; title page Peter Newark's Pictures; Pages: 4 AKG London/S Dominigie; 6 Peter Newark's Pictures; 7 AKG London/British Library; 8 AKG London/British Library; 9 Peter Newark's Pictures; 10 The Art Archive/Dagli Orti; 11 Peter Newark's Pictures; 12 AKG London; 14 Corbis/Lee Snider; 15 The Art Archive/Dagli Orti; 16 Corbis/Simone Martini; 17 The Art Archive; 18, 19, 20 AKG London; 21 AKG London/Stefan Diller; 23, 24 AKG London; 25 Corbis/Michael S. Yamashita; 26 Werner Forman Archives/Gulistan Imperial Library, Tehran; 27, 29 Scala; 31, 32 AKG London; 33 Werner Forman Archive; 34 Corbis/Bojan Brecelj; 35 The Art Archive; 36 AKG London; 37 Corbis/Burstein Collection; 38 Werner Forman Archive; 40 Corbis/AISA; 41 Corbis/Angelo Hornak; 42 Sonia Halliday Photographs/FHC Birch; 44 AKG London; 45 Scala; 46 Sylvia Cordaiy/Joy Whiting; 47 AKG London/Erich Lessing; 48 Sonia Halliday Photographs/Jane Taylor; 49 AKG London/Stefan Dreschel; 51 Corbis/Gianni Dagli Orti; 52 AKG London/Erich Lessing; 53, 54 AKG London; 55 Sonia Halliday Photographs; 56 AKG London; 57 Sylvia Cordaiy/Sheila Atter; 59 AKG London; 60 Peter Newark's Pictures; 61 AKG London/Erich Lessing; 62 Peter Newark Pictures; 63 AKG London; 65 The Art Archive; 66 Corbis/Phil Schemeister; 67 The Art Archive; 68 Sonia Halliday Photographs/Polly Buston.